# GOOD NEWS FOR A SUFFERING WORLD

D0808922

# ABOUT THE AUTHOR

Philip King studied Law at Oxford and Theology at Bristol.

He was ordained in 1960 and served in two suburban Church of England parishes in Surrey and south London.

In 1963 he married Margaret, a paediatrician. They have two daughters and two sons.

In 1968 he became Vicar of an inner city parish in west London.

From 1974 to 1986 he was General Secretary of the South American Missionary Society and was instrumental in setting up SAMS International, linking societies in Australia, Canada, Great Britain and Ireland, New Zealand and the Anglican Mission Association in South Africa. From 1982 to 1986 he was also a member of the international Mission Issues and Strategy Advisory Group of the Anglican Communion. Additionally in 1982 he became Chairman of the Mission Theology Advisory Group of the Board for Mission and Unity of the Church of England. The Group's first two publications were *The Measure of Mission* and *Good News in our Times – the Gospel and Contemporary Cultures*.

In 1986 he became Vicar of Christ Church and St Peter, Harrow, a multi-ethnic parish in north west London.

In 1989 he was made Secretary of the Church of England's Board for Mission and Unity and then on the division of the Board in April 1991 Secretary of the first Board of Mission.

In 1994 he also became Moderator of the Group for Evangelisation of Churches Together in England.

Philip King is also the author of *Making Christ Known* and *Leadership Explosion*.

# Good News for a Suffering World

*What does the Christian faith really have to offer?*

**PHILIP KING**

SCB Publishers

MONARCH
Crowborough

Copyright © Philip King 1996
The right of Philip King to be identified
as author of this work has been asserted by him in
accordance with the Copyright, Designs
and Patents Act 1988

First published 1996

All rights reserved.
No part of this publication may be reproduced or
transmitted in any form or by any means, electronic
or mechanical, including photocopy, recording or any
information storage and retrieval system, without
permission in writing from the publisher.

Unless otherwise stated, Scripture quotations are
taken from the Holy Bible, New International Version,
© 1973, 1978, 1984 by the International Bible Society.
Used by permission of Hodder and Stoughton Ltd.
All rights reserved.

**British Library Cataloguing Data**
A catalogue record for this book is available
from the British Library.

ISBN 1 85424 277 6

Co-published in South Africa with
SCB Publishers
Cornelis Struik House, 80 McKenzie Street
Cape Town 8001, South Africa
Reg no 04/02203/06

Designed and produced by Bookprint Creative Services
P.O. Box 827, BN21 3YJ, England for
MONARCH PUBLICATIONS
Broadway House, The Broadway
Crowborough, East Sussex, TN6 1HQ.
Printed in Great Britain.

# CONTENTS

# FOREWORD

One of the most heartening trends in the Church of England is the serious attention we are giving to evangelism. At one time this was not so; if we did not avoid the word we usually tried to find some way of denying its reality or we conspired to make it seem that it was the prerogative of a special interest group. Canon Philip King can justifiably claim some credit in giving mission and evangelism a more positive image. He has been at the centre of mission in the Church of England longer than he cares to remember and we are in his debt for his careful thought and faithful witness.

*Good News for a Suffering World* is a timely reminder that we should continue to wrestle with the theology of evangelism as well as the practice of making disciples. In this book Philip King skilfully weaves those twin themes together, drawing both on his experiences in this country and abroad, and on his theological reflections about Mission over many years. It is a book that challenges any tendencies towards superficial thinking as it wrestles with such questions as mission in the midst of suffering, relationships with those of other faiths and the links

7

between evangelism and social concern. I warmly commend this book for study and serious debate.

*George Cantuar*

ARCHBISHOP OF CANTERBURY
2 May 1996

# ACKNOWLEDGEMENTS

I am greatly indebted to a number of friends and especially to the Chairman, members and staff of the national Board of Mission of the Church of England for their encouragement, advice and critique in the writing of this book. The contents do not necessarily represent the views of the Board or of my colleagues, however, and are my responsibility. I am particularly grateful to my wife, family and colleagues for their patience and support. Special thanks are due to the Rev Dr Christopher Lamb, Dr Anne Richards, my personal assistant Kathryn Tye and Canon Robert Warren.

Philip King

# INTRODUCTION

*'"When I use a word," Humpty Dumpty said in a rather scornful tone, "it means just what I choose it to mean, neither more nor less."'*

An American missionary was travelling by car along a road in Brazil when a ragged man at the roadside thumbed a lift. Without slowing down the missionary tossed a copy of John's Gospel to the man through the car window. 'If he reads that,' he said to his companion, 'he may get converted, start doing an honest day's work and have a car of his own to ride around in.'

The story, a true one,[1] illustrates an extreme approach to evangelism and to suffering. The missionary clearly believed that social ills are primarily caused by individual sin. The answer to most social problems, therefore, is simply to seek the conversion of individuals and society will automatically be changed as a result.

The story of the missionary also raises questions about appropriate methods of evangelism and the nature of the God we proclaim. How far can the gospel effectively be shared unless Christians get alongside, listen to others and identify with their needs? How can we bring good news to a suffering world and proclaim a God who identified with the marginalised unless we do?

*The place of suffering*

The faith that we have to share is good news about peace, justice, and reconciliation, but the pathway to these benefits is often through suffering. Those undertaking reconciliation can often come under pressure, if not attack. The supreme example is Christ himself – 'Did not the Christ have to suffer these things and then enter his glory?' is the question put to the puzzled disciples on the road to Emmaus (Lk 24:26). For the apostles a call to evangelism meant a call to share in Christ's sufferings and to enter the sufferings of others (2 Cor 1:3–5). This is the root meaning of the word 'sympathy', to suffer (*pathos*) with (*sun*). Today the word sympathy can carry overtones of concern without commitment or even of condescension. Sympathy on its own is not enough,[2] but it is the right place to begin. We shall see how this theme of shared suffering can be extended to the whole of creation (page 99).

Several years ago I was travelling in a car driven by a missionary. The setting was Santiago in Chile just after the military coup and I was discussing with her the risks she had been taking as a doctor in giving treatment to left-wing activists, some of whom had been associated with Che Guevara. Soon after that another doctor, Sheila Cassidy, was imprisoned and tortured because she had given medical care to those considered to be enemies of the military regime.[3] Not many are called to experience this degree of suffering, but we are called to get involved with the needs of others, whatever the cost.

In March 1996, sixteen school children and their teacher were shot and killed in a Scottish primary school at Dunblane, while another twelve were injured. The mother of one of the children who escaped unharmed was chaplain to the local hospital, and in spite of the trauma she and others had suffered busied herself in counselling and comforting the injured and their relatives. 'Being in the places where people hurt most,' she said, 'is the only place to be.'

Methods of evangelism, sharing in suffering and a large number of other issues are tackled in this book. We shall be looking at the suffering of the world today (Chapter 1), at several 'good news words' that bring hope (Chapter 2), and then at the relation of evangelism to social needs (Chapter 3), to healing and suffering (Chapter 4), to culture (Chapter 5), to the church (Chapters 6 and 7), and to other faiths (Chapter 8). The chapters are designed in such a way that it is possible to take them in a different order: readers who want to start with the church, with culture or with other faiths are welcome to do so.

The Decade of Evangelism has spawned a large number of books on the 'how' of evangelism, but little on 'what' it is and still less on evangelism in the context of suffering. There has been an understandable fear that we could spend the whole Decade debating what we mean by evangelism and using the ensuing lack of agreement as an excuse for not doing it. There are, however, two opposite dangers – that of an extreme academic approach that undertakes theological reflection without engaging with people and their situations or their suffering, and that of the activists who are so busy with frenetic programmes of evangelism that they have no time to ask questions about the message and the appropriate methods. The answer is to combine action and reflection together and the following chapters seek to link practical examples with theological reflection. Material for discussion and action is provided at the end of the book.

In some ways theology is like reading a map. It is possible to enjoy a walking holiday without consulting a map, but the danger is that we walk round in circles or even fall over an unexpected cliff. On the other hand our understanding of the map has to be open to rethinking as we walk the terrain. There was once a curate who used an Ordnance Survey map to plan a youth club hike but didn't realise that what he thought was a footpath was in fact the county boundary. As the group panted up impossible inclines he was encouraged to look at the map again and to revise both his understanding and his approach.[4] This book is intended to give an outline map of evangelism in a suffering world, but one that is rooted in experience. Dr William Abraham has said that 'the great need in evangelism is not for some new programme, nor for a fresh wave of activism, but for a renewal of theological vision.'[5]

## How should we define evangelism?

One author has listed seventy-nine possible definitions.[6] Some of the more common ones include:

'Getting people into church'

'Making Christ Known' – the phrase used at the 1988 international Lambeth Conference of Anglican Bishops which called for a Decade of Evangelism

'Making Disciples' – as the hoped – for result of 'Making Christ Known'

'Transforming Society' – in justice and peace

The last definition is normally linked not so much with the word 'evangelism' but with 'evangelisation' – a word often used by Roman Catholics in the wider sense of describing the transformation of both society and individuals by the gospel. Protestants on the other hand tend to use the word 'mission' in this sense, and have often restricted 'evangelism' to the awakening of personal faith.[7] We shall see why this is unsatisfactory in Chapter 3.

It might be assumed that the debate could be settled by a quick reference to the New Testament. The immediate difficulty is that although the verb to evangelise (*evanggelizesthai*) appears fifty-two times and the word for gospel (*evanggelion*) seventy-two times, neither of the words 'evangelism' or 'evangelisation' appear as such. However any definition of 'evangelism' must refer to the activities and processes involved in sharing the gospel or good news. It must also be as comprehensive as the good news is; this means, for example, that there must be a social dimension to our definition of evangelism, a readiness to identify with suffering and need of every kind. This theme will be developed further in Chapter 3. Dr William Abraham's definition of 'initiating people into the kingdom of God'[8] has therefore much to commend it, though it has the disadvantage that it lacks an explicit reference to Christ.

A better phrase would be:

**Sharing the good news of Jesus Christ, together with his invitation to become his disciples, and to join with him in his work of transforming the world.**

Evangelism is not therefore an activity that stands apart from worship, discipling and social action, as illustrated in Figure 1, but is integral to them, as illustrated in Figures 2 and 3.

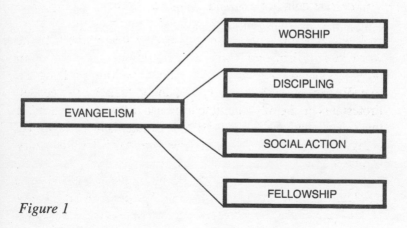

*Figure 1*

Figure 1 shows the traditional assumption that evangelism is a preliminary activity prior to and detached from other aspects of church life.

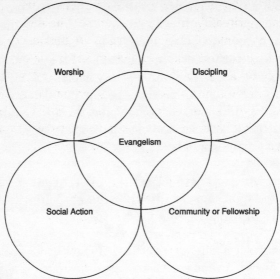

*Figure 2*

Figure 2 shows how evangelism is the announcing/inviting element that overlaps with other aspects of church life.

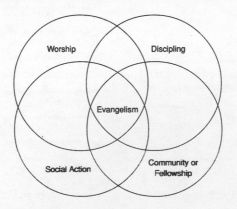

*Figure 3*

Figure 3 shows how all the elements overlap.

A missing dimension from these diagrams is the circle of prayer and spirituality. Spirituality can best be defined as the ways we encounter Christ and maintain that encounter. It clearly has a close link with evangelism and is one of the goals of making Christ known. After Saul's Damascus Road conversion, Ananias is told in a vision to go to a certain house and, 'ask for a man from Tarsus named Saul, *for he is praying*' (Acts 9:11). As a strict Pharisee Saul must have uttered many prayers, but this praying was a new experience from an encounter with Christ.

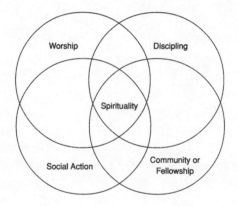

*Figure 4*[9]

Perhaps we need a three dimensional model, where Figure 4 above illustrates the inner counterpart, on the other side of the coin to Figure 3. Evangelism is the announcing and inviting dimension, and prayer and spirituality describe the resulting relationship.

## *Evangelists*

There are parallel questions concerning the definition of an evangelist. The word only appears three times in the New Testament – Acts 21:8, Eph 4:11 and 2 Tim 4:5 – and seems to have a different emphasis each time. On the first occasion it refers to Philip, a roving evangelist. On the second it refers to those who have an office within the church in order to equip church members for evangelism. The third occasion is where Paul exhorts Timothy, who also has roles of leadership, teaching and pastoral care, to do the work of an evangelist.

It can, however, be said that not every Christian has the gift and office of being an evangelist but that all have the responsibility to witness and to share the good news, ie, to evangelise. Where there is a reference to the work of an evangelist in the following pages, the principle can be applied in the majority of instances to the witness of every Christian.

## What does it matter?

There is a right and proper impatience with spending too much time on definitions. We may be tempted to identify with Humpty Dumpty and to say, 'When I use a word it means just what I choose it to mean, neither more nor less.' Because the New Testament does not give a definition, we can have a degree of flexibility in our modern definitions. But too great a flexibility does not make for clear communication and understanding. If a definition results in a narrowing down of the good news or in a distorted presentation of Jesus Christ, it should be challenged.

If our task is to share good news for a suffering world then it matters that we understand what that good news is. If Christ has sent us out into the world then it matters that we are clear about the task he has given us to do. If he has a vision of a new society and a new world then we must share that vision.

Yet while we need to question continually both the content and approach of our evangelism we should recognise that effectiveness in evangelism is not dependent on deep theological understanding – sometimes the reverse is true. The Acts of the Apostles portrays Peter and John as evangelists who led many thousands to faith, yet they are described by the theologians of the day as 'unschooled, ordinary men' (Acts 4:13).

We can be warned by the curate whose wife said, 'I used to understand his sermons before he went to college.' The answer is not, of course, to reject theology altogether but to seek a theology that is rooted and relevant to life.

Material for discussion and action on issues arising from the Introduction can be found on page 187.

## Notes

1. The story is told by Derek Winter in *Hope in Captivity* (Epworth Press: London, 1977), p 20.
2. A recent report on the homeless by the London Churches Group was entitled, 'From Sympathy to Solidarity' (London Churches Group, City Temple, Holborn Viaduct, London EC1A 2OE).
3. The story is told by Sheila Cassidy in *Audacity to Believe* (Darton Longman & Todd: London, 1977).
4. The story is told by Tom Walker in *Renew Us by Your Spirit* (Hodder: London, 1982), p 132.
5. William Abraham, *The Logic of Evangelism* (Hodder: London, 1982), p 114.
6. David Barrett, *World Christian Encyclopedia* (OUP: Nairobi, 1987), pp 42–45.
7. This is the definition of evangelism used in a paper written by the Rev Donald Elliott, Secretary of the Churches' Commission on Mission of the Council of Churches for Britain and Ireland, Inter-Church House, 35 Lower Marsh, London SE1 7RL.
8. Abraham, *op cit*, p 95.
9. A similar diagram is used by Canon Robert Warren in *Building Missionary Congregations* (Church House Publishing: London, 1995), p 20.

# CHAPTER ONE

# WHAT HOPE FOR PLANET EARTH?

*World Trends and Counter Trends*

One way of distinguishing an optimist from a pessimist is to compare their approaches to a ring doughnut – the optimist sees the doughnut and the pessimist the hole. As we look at today's world we need the attitude not of the optimist or the pessimist, but of the realist who sees both doughnut and hole, both threats and signs of hope.

Before developing the theme of 'Good News for a Suffering World' it is important to focus on the world in which that good news is to be shared. What are the problems and the possibilities? In what ways can we speak of a 'suffering world'? What aspects of the good news are relevant to each need?

Of necessity this has to be a rapid introductory survey with a minimum of detail. It is designed to highlight the issues that will be discussed later in the book. It raises questions rather than at this stage providing answers. First I want to list a number of general global trends. These interlock as illustrated in Figure 5.

## General global trends

Commentators can find plenty of justification for prophecies of gloom and doom. Many are doubting whether 'planet earth' has a future – at least as regards human life as we know it. The major

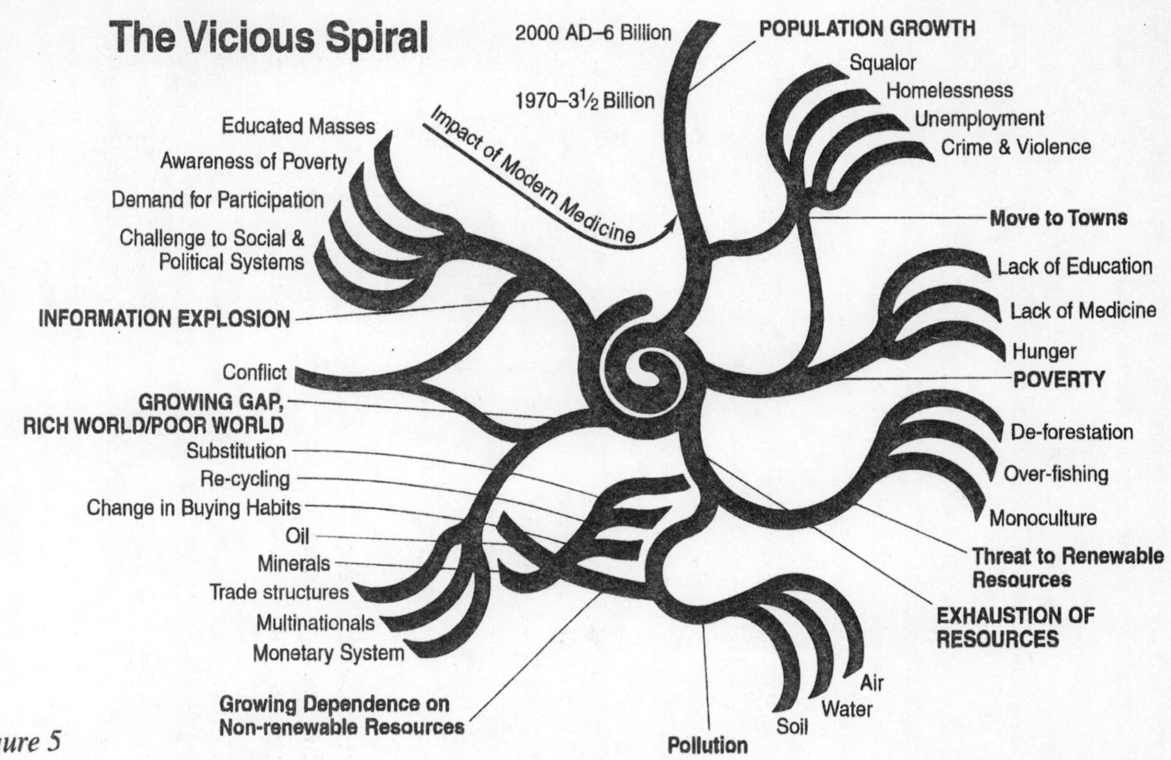

# The Vicious Spiral

POPULATION GROWTH
- 2000 AD—6 Billion
- 1970—3½ Billion

Squalor
Homelessness
Unemployment
Crime & Violence

**Move to Towns**

Lack of Education
Lack of Medicine
Hunger
**POVERTY**

De-forestation
Over-fishing
Monoculture
**Threat to Renewable Resources**

**EXHAUSTION OF RESOURCES**

Air
Water
Soil

**Pollution**

Impact of Modern Medicine

Educated Masses
Awareness of Poverty
Demand for Participation
Challenge to Social & Political Systems

**INFORMATION EXPLOSION**

Conflict
**GROWING GAP, RICH WORLD/POOR WORLD**
Substitution
Re-cycling
Change in Buying Habits
Oil
Minerals
Trade structures
Multinationals
Monetary System

**Growing Dependence on Non-renewable Resources**

Figure 5

problems include growth in population, poverty and pollution. As we draw near to a new millennium there will undoubtedly be religious groups prophesying that 'the end is nigh'. There were plenty of doom-laden predictions in the run-up to the year 1,000 and there are likely to be many more as we enter the Third Millennium.

But there are sound scientific reasons for fear and disquiet. Even in 1975 Professor Charles Birch, speaking at the World Council of Churches Assembly in Nairobi, described the world as being like the *Titanic*, on a course heading for destruction, but with the richer passengers wining and dining, seemingly oblivious to danger. Today there is a greater awareness of the dangers ahead, but not one that is matched with action – we could say the passengers are now 'whining and dining'.

Against this sombre background there are signs of hope, shining like stars on a dark night. These signs of hope can be illustrated by two pieces of television footage that will long be remembered – the jubilant crowd hammering down the concrete slabs of the Berlin wall, and more recently the victorious South African Rugby Team, winners of the 1995 World Cup, standing in a circle with their heads bowed in a prayer of thanksgiving. They were symbols of a country that had achieved a miracle of reconciliation. Whatever the gloom, there are shining stars of hope.

## Conflict and war

But we must begin with the gloom. Although communism in Eastern Europe has collapsed and the Cold War has ended, a whole range of different problems are emerging. Recent events in the Gulf, Rwanda and Bosnia are a sad reminder that wars, conflicts and 'ethnic cleansing' are still with us, and that unscrupulous leaders may get access to terrible weapons and wreak havoc. How can the gospel message of reconciliation be made relevant to such conflicts, especially in a country like

Rwanda which has been famous for its experience of revival?

## Growth in population and poverty

The forecast of population growth is frightening. The present world population figure is already over 5 billion; it is estimated that this figure could double by the middle of the twenty-first century. One result will inevitably be an increase in the demand for food and other resources. But already there is an acute shortage of food in parts of the world, with many experiencing starvation or malnutrition. Those who suffer malnutrition have a lower resistance to disease. Every day 40,000 children die from malnutrition and common diseases, an equivalent of 14 million per year.[1]

Population growth leads to poverty and food shortage, but there is also an inverse link between population and poverty. It has been shown that poorer families tend to have more children; this is partly due to the need for an extra pair of hands to cultivate the land, and partly because of high infant mortality rates and low life expectancy. Parents who fear that some of their children will fail to survive understandably want to have more. There are also cultural and religious factors, such as the attitude to birth control, that have a direct effect on population growth.

But population growth is not the only cause of poverty. This can be demonstrated by the fact that the population of the United Kingdom per square kilometre is 50% higher than that of India. Over-population is everybody's baby. A significant factor causing poverty in India is that the country has not experienced the same degree of industrial 'development' as has the UK – for a long period its economy was dominated by the power of the East India Company. Although the colonial era brought some positive gains, such as education and medicine, there was a tendency to encourage the development of products that benefitted the colonial powers rather than the country concerned – in the case of India it was tea and coffee.

## Urbanisation

Growth in population and poverty has led to a rapid increase in urbanisation. One estimate is that São Paulo could soon reach 28 million and Mexico City 32 million. Third World cities tend to be ringed by expanding shanty towns. Peasants in the countryside tune in on their transistor radios and hear of the goods on offer in the cities and move in. They hope to find the streets paved with gold but find they are not paved at all. They are sucked into a poverty trap, with no work and no land where they can scratch a living.

## Pollution and exhaustion of the earth's resources

Most of the global trends in the first part of this chapter are interconnected. Growth in population and poverty can and often does lead to over-cultivation, destruction of forests, soil erosion, pollution and exhaustion of resources. The 'greenhouse effect' of higher levels of carbon dioxide in the atmosphere may lead to higher temperatures, partial melting of the polar ice caps, raising of ocean levels and widespread flooding.

A major factor behind increased carbon dioxide is the destruction of the world's rain forests. At one extreme we have the starving peasant scratching a living and needing to cut down trees in order to have a wood fire. At the other extreme we have the commercial company clearing vast tracts of land to establish new cattle ranches or to develop agriculture. Over two-thirds of India's forests have been lost in this century. Increase in population and poverty lead in turn to over-cultivation. In some areas of the world this has led to soil erosion: the Sahara desert, for example, is growing year by year. It has been well said that, 'Civilised man has marched across the face of the earth and left a desert in his footprints.'[2] How long will it be before the Sahara desert leaps the Mediterranean?

All these factors lead to the exhaustion of the earth's resources, such as coal and oil.

How far does our understanding of the good news extend to the environment? We shall see on page 46 that it can and should.

## 'Now we know we're poor'

Meanwhile radio and television have brought the whole world to everyone's living rooms. The 'have nots' become aware of how much the 'haves' possess. Shanty-town dwellers have always been poor, but now they know how poor they are. There is a similar effect in the West.[3] Although poverty here is not on a third-world scale, those living in relative poverty are made aware of the growing gap. Through television adverts they are daily presented with attractive goods that they cannot afford to buy.

## A widening gap

There is evidence that the gap between the rich and the poor is growing. This is true of the gap between rich and poor nations such as the USA and India, but there is also a widening gap between rich and poor individuals within nations, both in the Third World and elsewhere. In Britain it has been argued that the number of people with incomes below 50% of the national average income has risen from 5 million in 1979 to 13.9 million in 1992. In 1979 the poorer half of the population received one third of total income, but this has now fallen to one quarter.[4] In 1995 it was argued that it would take a British Gas showroom assistant 100 years to earn what the chairman, then Cedric Brown, could accumulate with the help of share options in one year.

The gap between the North and the South[5] is exacerbated by crippling international debt. Banks encouraged Third World countries to borrow at low interest, but then world interest rates shot up, partly to meet the domestic needs of the United States. Many Third-World countries now pay more in interest than they receive in aid. Since 1987 sub-Saharan African countries have paid £1.10 to rich countries in debt repayments for every £1 received in loans. Spending on health care in Uganda is about £1.60 per person, compared with £19 spent on debt repayments. Such is the problem that the Pope has called for the remission of international debt in the year 2000 as a 'sign of jubilee'.[6] Cancelling the debt of most indebted African countries is possible without harming the global economy – sub-Saharan African debt amounts to only 1% of world trade.

*Violence*

In some countries the widening gap leads to an increase in crime and violence. Those using the New York subway will find an area of the platform patrolled by armed guards; passengers can wait there in relative safety. In Rio tourists staying at some hotels are placed on the beach in the care of guardians with revolvers – such is the incidence of armed robbery. So many security measures are needed for the homes of the relatively wealthy in São Paulo that it has been said that the rich shelter in fortresses while the poor huddle in *favelas*.

Current trends in population growth, poverty, pollution and exhaustion of resources, coupled with better communication, become a vicious spiral leading to growing tension and conflict.


## The disappearance of hope

When Bishop Lesslie Newbigin returned to Britain after decades as a missionary in India he was asked what was the most dramatic change he had noticed in his homeland. 'The disappearance of hope,' he replied.[7] Even in the worst slums in Madras there is hope that things can be better. The Enlightenment and the Industrial Revolution had inspired the utopian hope that the human race was on a continuous course of improvement. The development of medicine, education, science and technology gave every expectation of steady progress. This optimism was shattered in the twentieth century by two World Wars and the development of nuclear weapons. Forty million people died in the Second World War alone. It became clear that science and technology could be used with increasing efficiency to destroy life as well as to save it. As Winston Churchill put it in a speech to the House of Commons in 1950:

> Man in this moment of his history has emerged in greater supremacy over the forces of nature than has ever been dreamed of before. He has it in his power to solve quite easily the problems of material existence. He has conquered the wild beasts, and he has even conquered the insects and the microbes. There lies before him, if he wishes, a golden age of peace and progress. All is in his hand. He has only to conquer his last and worst enemy – himself.

During the 1950s, however, some of the optimism revived. The British public were told by Prime Minister Harold Macmillan, 'You've never had it so good.' This was also the 'development era' when it was expected that Third World countries could and should imitate, with first-world help, the industrial 'development' of the North. With the exception of some countries on the Pacific Rim this has not proved possible.[8] Meanwhile in the literature and the arts of the West there was a growing despair; so much so that the Chinese theologian Carver Yu described Western culture as containing 'technological optimism and literary despair.'[9] Then there came growing unemployment, the collapse of communism and increasing disenchantment with capitalism. It became clear that technology did not have all the answers.

If we are to speak of 'Good News for a Suffering World' we have to know something about the needs of the world and of what the Christian faith has to offer. The good news of how the Spirit of God enters into the sufferings of men and women and of the creation in order to transform both humanity and the environment is described in chapter 4 (page 99).

## Signs of hope

There are however many signs of hope, demonstrating God at work in the world. We have already mentioned the miraculous changes in South Africa and Eastern Europe. Many of the world's leaders seem to be talking to each other in a significantly different way, though there continue to be many setbacks in the progress towards peace and harmony.

Furthermore, many world trends can have positive as well as negative results. The information explosion brought about through radio, television and computer highways results in the poor being more aware of their plight, but it also makes others aware and can generate a partnership of concern, demonstrated in such projects as 'Comic Relief' and 'Live Aid'. George Orwell, in his book *1984*, thought of television as a tool for oppression; every citizen was watched by 'Big Brother'. But at its best it can be a means of challenging government authorities and multi-national companies. Media coverage has made possible the growth of networks such as Greenpeace and Amnesty International. It has shown how dedicated campaigners in small boats can challenge the might of naval flotillas. Figures like Mother Teresa, Desmond Tutu and Nelson Mandela have become internationally famous and are beacons of hope. National and international communication will undoubtedly be significantly increased through the Internet.

There has even been some success with the intractable problems of population, poverty and pollution; the doom merchants may be proved wrong in their timing if not in the final scenario. Perhaps the cartoonist is right who portrayed a sandwich board saying in large letters 'The End is Nigh' – underneath, however, he added in smaller letters, 'But I could be wrong.'

With international agreement and the right degree of political goodwill and courage, resources could be devoted to tackling today's problems of poverty and pollution. It would be costly, but it is unlikely to need the vast sums devoted to the arms race during the Cold War.

One example of hope comes from the fact that a link has been discovered between a rise in education for women and a drop in the birthrate. In Brazil the birthrate dropped from 4.7 children per woman in the period 1970–1975 to 3.5 children per woman in the period 1983–1986.

There are examples of significant improvements in agricultural yields and of tackling pollution. Globally cereal production has been rising on average at a rate of about 1% per annum. Africa had a 23% rise comparing the period 1976–1978 and 1986–1988, though the rise was outpaced by population growth. Many towns and regions in Europe and North America are now environmentally a good deal more pleasant to inhabit.

But it would be rash to dismiss these global problems as being easy to solve. Few voters and fewer politicians are prepared to make significant sacrifices for future generations.

## Specific trends and counter-trends

We have already seen how the information explosion can produce positive as well as negative results. The same is true of a number of other current trends. The following six couples show how a tendency in one direction is often countered by a counter-trend in the opposite one. Again this has to be a rapid survey with a minimum of detail at this point, though many of the issues will surface again in later chapters.

### 1. Centralisation yet fragmentation

Technological progress has led to increasing centralisation and to the growth of large multi-national companies who can switch production lines from one country to another. If car workers fought for better pay in England the cars could be made in Spain. One English clothes chain has its garments made up in the Arab Emirates. This provides employment in the Emirates and also keeps labour costs down.

Centralisation can sometimes lead to greater efficiency, innovation and reduction of costs, but the downside can be a feeling of remoteness and lack of accountability. For many people the sense of powerlessness has increased. Everything always seems to be decided somewhere else. The Scottish and Welsh have often felt that their lives are dominated by decisions taken in Westminster or the City of London, but today they and Londoners find that decisions have been made in New York, Brussels, or Tokyo. Life has become so complex that those who invest or take out life insurance often have little knowledge of how their money is being used.

Recently an elderly couple effectively evicted themselves from their retirement home. They had invested their savings in a large commercial company. The company then invested some of its capital, including the couple's savings, with a property developer who decided to buy up the block of flats where they lived. To make good use of the capital the developer then evicted the tenants and pulled the block down.

Reference has been made earlier to the disparity between the income of the chairman of British Gas and the wages of showroom assistants. A number of small shareholders tried to challenge the position at the annual meeting but were outvoted by the large company shareholders. It may well be that some of the small shareholders had, unknown to them, some of their savings invested with the companies concerned.

One of the reactions against political and economic centralisation has been a growing fragmentation. The fall of communism has led to the reassertion of national and ethnic identities in the former Soviet Union and in former Yugoslavia, with tragic results. There are examples of fragmentation within industry and government services, too. Whatever the pros and cons of privatisation the argument for the break up of monopolies and for some of the changes in the British education and health services is that of subsidiarity – that decisions should be pushed down to as local a level as possible. The same has happened within large companies in the United States, Britain and Australia.

As with many of the trends described in this section there is potential for both good and bad. A new sense of identity and belonging is important when technology and economics tend to anonymity and remoteness. Both in the church and society we need structures that provide for the possibility of local identity and participation while at the same time recognising the need for wider networks of cooperation.

## 2. Depersonalisation yet individualism

Complicated industrial and technological societies tend to depersonalise. The person becomes a PIN number for the banks and a body on the hospital ward; the development of medical techniques may not be accompanied by personal skills at the bedside. The ultimate depersonalisation came when a local authority in west London decided to reorganise the town cemetery and decreed that the tombstones in its cemetery should no longer display the name of the deceased and a message from relatives, but simply a five-figure reference number; the name of the occupant of the anonymous grave could be discovered by reporting the reference number to the cemetery office. Fortunately the policy was changed after protests.

The trend towards greater mechanisation in industry has increased the sense of powerlessness. As companies have introduced mechanisation they have drastically reduced their workforce. Those remaining in work find they are under increasing pressure – fewer people are in work, but those who are have to work harder. People are either discarded or driven by capitalism.

However, there has been a reaction against centralisation, depersonalisation and a sense of being of little worth or value in the form of a growing individualism. Again this has both positive and negative features. There has been a healthy emphasis on the importance and rights of the individual. The individual matters, and concern for equality has broken down many of the barriers of race, class and gender. Our era has been described as the 'me' generation with the call to 'be good to yourself'. Again this has its positive side; we are to love our neighbours as ourselves and therefore being good to ourselves is appropriate. But sometimes the call to be good to ourselves carries the implication that others don't matter. It has been used as a justification for getting out of an unhappy marriage in cases where the difficulties might have been overcome through patience and counselling. The importance of the individual is sometimes emphasised as against the family or the local community. Indeed the modern family has been described as 'a collection of individuals round a television set'. In some homes individualism has been taken a stage further with television sets and computers in separate rooms.

In many areas there is little community life left. Baroness Margaret Thatcher, during her time as Prime Minister of Great Britain, even questioned whether there was any such thing as society.

Good news for our modern society needs to take the individual seriously, giving each person worth and value, yet at the same time emphasising the importance of relationships and community.

## 3. Detachment yet engagement

The increase in television channels and viewing hours has made us better informed, but can also create a 'spectator society'. We can sit in an armchair in Australia and watch people starve in Africa. During the Gulf War viewers in the United States and elsewhere were able to watch missiles pierce buildings in Baghdad. War was being covered in a way not unlike the screening of a football match. But the only way we can cope with the conflicts, violence and horrors bombarding us daily through the screen is to develop a degree of detachment. Unfortunately this attitude pervades other spheres of life. In 1995 two girls were attacked by a group of boys on a suburban train in the north of England. The other passengers did nothing to help and just watched. There are a number of instances in Britain and the USA where passers-by have simply walked past a person lying ill or injured on the pavement or sidewalk.

The phenomenon of detachment means a drop in support for most institutional meetings, whether those of the churches or of political parties.

But this is not true of everyone. Specialist interest groups and campaigning bodies such as Greenpeace and Amnesty International are on the increase. For some the reaction to our complex centralised world is fight, not flight, engagement not detachment. This ought to be true of the Christian. Evangelism that presents Christ's invitation to discipleship should include a call to become committed to the kind of engagement with the world and its problems that he modelled.

## 4. Transience yet a search for roots

We live in what has been described as an 'era of accelerated change'.[10] In order to maximise profits companies continually have to produce new models and new lines. Today's car is obsolete tomorrow. This year's fashions are out of date in the next. Companies merge or go out of business much more frequently than in an earlier generation. Production is switched from one area to another. In the first half of the century it was not unusual for those joining a company in their teens to expect to stay until retirement. Today such stability would be regarded at a job interview as a lack of ambition and vision.

Transience is a factor in the home as well as the work-place. Cohabitation as a prelude to or a substitute for marriage is now commonplace. Many of those who marry do not see it as a commitment for life; with increasing divorce the pattern is a form of polygamy described as 'serial monogamy'. It can be argued that there are cases where the break up of a marriage may be a lesser evil than the continuance of a relationship that is damaging to both parents and children, and that some of those who advocate a return to 'Victorian values' overlook the problems that lay hidden in many Victorian homes. But there is evidence that the degree of transience in modern relationships creates significant insecurity if not damage to both adults and children.

As a reaction to constant change and its demands there is an increasing 'search for roots'. Many have taken up the hobby of constructing their 'family tree'. Period dramas on television are increasingly popular, and many produced in Britain are marketed in the States and Australia. Thousands go on pilgrimage to cathedrals and other historic sites.

This search for roots gives particular opportunities for historic churches, provided they do not become museums where people seek refuge from a changing world. But the trend towards transience faces the churches with problems. How can we balance tradition and stability with flexibility? Church-goers increasingly move from one church to another or think of regular attendance as once or twice a month.

## 5. Secularisation yet spirituality

The general trend in the West is towards secularisation in the sense of being ignorant of the Christian faith or not practising it. Although in Britain over 75% claim to believe in God, only 10% of the population attend church. In the United States church attendance is over 40%, but in New Zealand only 16%. It cannot be assumed today that the average person in the West has as much knowledge of the Christian faith as previous generations did. Many school children will not have heard of the 'Good Samaritan' and a recent international survey revealed that 88% of those surveyed recognised the golden arches symbol used by the McDonald's fast food chain, but only 54% knew what a cross symbolised.[11]

Yet secularisation has left a vacuum and there is a hunger for spirituality or an encounter with 'something beyond'. For some this means an encounter with the Christian God. The numbers of those wishing to go on retreats or to visit a Christian community such as Taizé is on the increase. One of the Taizé brothers spoke recently of the thirst among people for spiritual experience. For others the attraction will be New Age or one of the New Religious Movements such as 'the Moonies' or 'The Church of Scientology'. As G K Chesterton is quoted as saying, 'when people stop believing in God it is not that they believe in nothing, rather they believe in anything.' In part this is a reaction to the materialism of both communism and capitalism, and to the secular 'certainties' of science and technology that have been found wanting.

## 6. Rejection of authority yet fundamentalism

For several generations we have been taught to question and argue in the classroom. Statements are no longer taken on trust from 'authority figures', with the exception of pop idols or leading sports players. At its best this is healthy – truth has to be discovered by each individual as a result of dialogue and exploration. At its worst, however, it can lead to the kind of cynicism that imputes false motives to every public leader.

It is often said that we live in a pluralist society where there are a number of beliefs coexisting side by side. The term 'university' was meant to imply a coherent overarching body of truth; a more accurate phrase today would be 'pluriversity'! Pluralism for some means relativism – a belief that everything is relative and that there is no such thing as ultimate truth. The one exception, that demonstrates the inherent weakness of this position, is the statement that there is no such thing as ultimate truth! For the relativist there are few, if any, moral absolutes. Morals are more a matter of individual choice.

The result has been a moral vacuum. In practice, of course, there is no shortage of implicit values that are assumed, sometimes without question or recognition. One example is the value system of the market place – the belief that if something is not 'economic' it is bad. The dangers of this vacuum were highlighted by the Jamie Bulger case, where a small boy was picked up by two older boys in a market place in the north of England, taken to a railway line and killed. A good deal of national soul-searching took place as a result and questions were asked as to how far society can function without parents teaching children moral values.

There will be fuller discussion of pluralism, relativism, secularisation and postmodernism in Chapter 7.

A significant counter-trend to this rejection of authority has been a search for new authority figures in society, politics and the church and a rise of Christian, Muslim and other forms of fundamentalism or extremism.

The word 'fundamentalism' is not being used here in the good sense of a concern for the fundamentals of a faith, but in the popular sense of the kind of extremism that is not open to considering other points of view.

There have been several examples of people being prepared to follow cult leaders to their death – one of the worst was the series of events at Waco in Texas, where many cult disciples died in a fire after barricading themselves into their headquarters.

## Hope, God and the church

Sometimes some of the signs of hope are brought about and demonstrated in and through the life of the church. Christians have played a significant role in the changes that have occurred in South Africa and in the former communist countries in Eastern Europe. Individual Christians are members, too, of secular networks such as Amnesty International and Greenpeace. We need to remember that God loves the world (Jn 3:16) not just the church and is active in the world both in areas where there is a Christian presence and in areas where there is not.

We must be careful to proclaim a God and a gospel that is big enough for today's world. The trouble is, as Bishop Maurice Sinclair has put it, 'Many Christians do not see a vital connection between Christian mission and the confrontation of world problems.'[12] One of the tasks of this book is to make the connection and to demonstrate what the Christian faith has to offer in bringing good news to a suffering world. Some of the elements of that good news are expounded in the next chapter.

Issues from this chapter for discussion and action will be found on page 187.

## Notes

1. Ben Jackson, *Poverty and the Planet* (Penguin: London, 1990), p 31.
2. E F Schumacher, *Small is Beautiful* (Abacus: London, 1974), p 84.
3. I have followed the custom of using the word 'South' to describe the Third- or two-thirds world, and 'the West' to describe Europe, North America, Australia, New Zealand and South Africa. Latin America is included in the 'South' and not the West.
4. Newsletter of Church Action on Poverty (August 1994): Central Buildings, Oldham Street, Manchester M1 1JT
5. See note 3 above. I have followed the custom of using the word 'North' as virtually coterminous with the 'West'.
6. The Old Testament custom of 'jubilee' was to command remission of debts every jubilee or fifty years.
7. *Windows on Salvation* ed. Donald English (Darton, Longman & Todd: London, 1994), p 148.
8. Many of the reasons for this are expounded by Paul Kennedy in his book *Preparing for the Twenty-first Century* (Fontana: London, 1994). Paul gives fascinating comparisons between countries on the Pacific Rim and elsewhere.

9. Martin Robinson, *The Faith of the Unbeliever* (Monarch: Crowborough, 1994), p 16.
10. Alvin Toffler, *Future Shock* (Bodley Head: London, 1970)
11. This survey was conducted by Sponsorship Research International among 7,000 people in Britain, Germany, the USA, India, Japan and Australia. The facts quoted were published in the *Daily Mail* on 20 July 1995.
12. Maurice Sinclair, *Ripening Harvest, Gathering Storm* (MARC: Eastbourne, 1988), p 120.

# CHAPTER TWO

# GOOD NEWS FOR A NEW MILLENNIUM

*Words of Hope for a Suffering World*

Many of the walls on the housing estate at the edge of the city were covered with graffiti, the phone boxes had been wrecked and people were afraid to go out at night for fear of being mugged. There were very few premises available for social or community events, and what there was had been vandalised. Worst of all was the feeling of hopelessness in the air. 'The main deprivation here,' said a clergyman working on the estate, 'is lack of hope.'

Is there any way we can make a connection between the problems on this housing estate and the hope promised through the gospel? The first letter of Peter describes the task of evangelism in terms of sharing good news of hope – 'Always be prepared to give an answer to everyone who asks you a reason for the hope that you have' (1 Pet 3:15). But what forms of good news can be relevant to this part of a suffering world?

On the one hand lies the danger of a simplistic answer; 'Come to Christ and all your problems will be solved.' On the other hand it is of limited help to seek answers that have no reference to the Christian faith. An essay published in 1995 on the needs of Urban Priority Areas said, 'Is it not also striking how a great deal of Christian discussion, analysis and activity in these areas seems to have little or no living relation to the basic Christian activity of worship, or even to have no reference to God?'[1]

The focus and the foundation of hope for the Christian is the life, death and resurrection of Jesus Christ, and the most basic definition of evangelism is that of sharing the good news of Christ. A Church of England report on Mission and Evangelism put it this way – 'We are charged to communicate that the life, death and resurrection of Jesus Christ is good news from God.'[2]

How can our evangelism relate to the various contexts in which people live today? How can we share good news that will be relevant in a new millennium? This is the theme running through the whole of this book, but this chapter begins to explore a number of 'gospel' or 'hope' words that give us clues as to how the links can be made.

The first is:

*Identification*

We saw in Chapter 1 that many today lack a sense of self-worth or value. This may result from trauma in childhood, from a breakdown in a relationship, from unemployment or redundancy or from a variety of other factors. Even those who have a job, a home and a stable relationship can feel powerless, at the mercy of distant social or economic forces over which they seem to have little or no control. However we have a God who in Christ voluntarily surrendered his security and power and became vulnerable. It is interesting to speculate whether Jesus could have fulfilled his mission through being born in a palace and by being brought up in a safe environment, but he chose to be identified with the poor and the marginalised of society. For him every individual mattered and had worth and value. He spent a high proportion of his three-year ministry in training twelve men, one of whom was to betray him.

Words such as identification and incarnation are a reminder that our God has shared our suffering and in his resurrected humanity still does. The model to use from the Introduction is that of Dr Sheila Cassidy and the other missionary doctor – not that of the missionary who seemed to have insulated himself from suffering.

## Welcome and acceptance

These words flow naturally from the ideas of identification and incarnation. Jesus identified with and was willing to welcome those rejected by the society of his day – Zacchaeus, Mary Magdalene, and many others.

One of the most famous parables of Jesus is that of the prodigal son (Lk 15). The story graphically demonstrates that however much we have wasted God's resources and spoilt his environment, however much we have turned our back on him and preferred to try and enjoy life on our own, he is always willing to welcome and receive us back, if we repent and return. The jealousy and ingratitude displayed by the older brother, who represents some among the religious leadership of that day, is a reminder that those who are outwardly closer to God may be further away in their hearts.

As Paul Tillich has put it, 'Accept that you have been accepted, despite being unacceptable.'[3] Christ is willing to accept us however 'unacceptable' we are. Dr Simon Chan, an Assemblies of God pastor in Singapore, has described this acceptance in terms of accessibility and openness.[4] We are invited into the presence of Christ – he is always accessible. He calls us his friends and lets us into his secrets – 'a servant does not know his master's business. Instead I have called you friends for everything I have learnt from my Father I have made known to you' (Jn 15:15).

But the corollary of God's acceptance of us is that we should be willing to accept others. Paul expresses it in these words – 'Accept one another, then, just as Christ accepted you' (Rom 15:7).

A common symbol of acceptance in Jewish culture was an invitation to a meal. Meals, feasts and celebrations were central to Judaism; examples are the Passover and the Feast of Weeks at Pentecost. Jesus made many of his contacts at meal tables: he would frequently accept invitations to dine with Pharisees and was invited by the converted tax collector Levi to meet his friends over a meal. Such was his stress on celebration that he was accused of being over-fond of wine.

The slogan over the Communion Table in one church was 'This man receives sinners and eats with them,' implying that no one is to be rejected. The only people 'unworthy' to come to the Lord's Table are those unwilling to admit their sin and their need of Christ's forgiveness.

One of the biggest divisions in first-century Palestine was that between Jews and non-Jews or Gentiles: Jews were not allowed to eat with Gentiles. A critical issue for the early church therefore was whether Gentile Christians could share a meal with Christians from a Jewish background: it was agreed after debate (Acts 15) that such acceptance was central to the gospel, though at one point Paul had to criticise Peter for going back on the agreement (Gal 2:11). This principle of acceptance is central today in bringing healing and hope in a divided and suffering world. Because God accepts us as we are, and not on any ground of status or worth, so we can accept others and be accepted ourselves. Acceptance is the secret of giving a sense of worth, value and identity to those who feel powerless and devalued in modern society. The congregation at Corinth did not have many members who had status in term of intellect, influence or birth (1 Cor 1:26) but in Christ they were given wisdom and status as sons and daughters of God.

This was graphically illustrated in a church meeting in Chile, a country where social divisions have been particularly strong. An upper-class professional woman and a maid living in a shanty town wept with joy as they embraced each other during 'the peace' at a diocesan Communion service. In everyday social settings, such an experience would have been impossible

– it is unlikely that they would even have been sitting at the same table, let alone embracing one another.

## Reconciliation and forgiveness

Where there has been estrangement and alienation there has to be reconciliation and forgiveness before there can be welcome and acceptance. The focal point of our forgiveness is the cross, where Christ welcomed the penitent thief and prayed for forgiveness for those who had crucified him. 'God was in Christ reconciling the world to himself, not counting their trespasses against them' (2 Cor 5:19 RSV).

There are at least two dimensions in which reconciliation is needed. Provided we do not take the terms literally they can be described as the vertical dimension between men and women and God, and the horizontal one, between individuals, groups and nations. Once a relationship is broken in one dimension, relationships in other dimensions can be affected. A business-man or woman who has had a frustrating day at the office may come home, scowl at their spouse, swear at the children and kick the cat. In a similar way, the vertical and horizontal dimensions can affect each other, too. Christ warned that our offerings will be unacceptable to God unless we are first reconciled with a brother we have wronged (Mt 5:23–24). God will not listen to us if we are not listening to others. On the other hand, if we have turned away from God and have failed to seek his forgiveness then our horizontal relationships will be spoiled.

The following verses describe how Jews and Gentiles can be reconciled through the cross:

> 'He himself is our peace, who has made the two one . . . by abolishing in his flesh the law with its commandments and regulations. His purpose was to create in himself one new man out of the two, thus making peace, and in this one body to reconcile both of them to God through the cross . . . He came and preached peace to you

who were far away and peace to those who are near . . .' (Eph 2:14–18).

The 'two' here are the Jews and the Gentiles. Although the Ten Commandments are still important guidelines for Christian living, the death of Christ has abolished law-keeping as a means of winning God's favour: men and women can no longer claim that God accepts them on the basis of living a good life in accordance with God's commands. By that standard we all fall short, whether Jew or Gentile. Both Jew and Gentile can therefore be accepted by faith on the grounds of the cross. One of the favourite phrases of the East African revival was that 'there is level ground at Calvary', none of us can stand taller than others before God. There can now therefore be peace between Jew and Gentile, between every race and nation, and between women and men and God. Before the cross, pride of nationality, race, social position, wealth or education are rendered meaningless. The 'new man' or 'new humanity' being created in and by the Holy Spirit transcends all these divisions.

This was illustrated by Jesus in his encounter with the Samaritan woman at the well. There was such division and hatred between Jews and Samaritans that Jews would not use the same drinking vessels. Yet Jesus was prepared to ask the Samaritan woman for a drink.

In 1995 the Netherlands hosted a special conference to celebrate the 50th anniversary of liberation from the Nazi regime at the end of the Second World War. The prepared agenda was abandoned as German and Dutch Christians were reconciled at a deep level. Similar reports came from a conference the same year in Seoul where Japanese knelt before Koreans, and Arabs embraced Jewish Christians.

*Peace*

Many of the themes illustrated by our list of 'gospel words' overlap and this is especially true of 'reconciliation' and 'peace'. The word peace is highlighted in the quotation from Ephesians 2 in the section above.

There have been more wars this century than at any other period in history. Apart from the conflicts we describe as the two 'World Wars' we have seen war in Vietnam, the Gulf, Sudan and Bosnia, to name just a few. Since 1500 BC there have been over 8,000 treaties of peace; each one has been in force for an average of two years! A concern to make and maintain peace is bound, therefore, to be high on most agendas.

'Peace' is one of the themes associated with the coming Messiah in the prophet Isaiah. He is described as 'the Prince of Peace' whose rule will result in swords being reshaped into ploughshares – weapons of destruction become tools to provide for the needy (Is 9:6 and 2:4). This theme is taken up by St Peter who describes the gospel as 'good news of peace through Jesus Christ, who is Lord of all' (Acts 10:36). One of the keys to peace is submission to the rule of Christ as Lord.

The word for peace in the Old Testament – *Shalom* in Hebrew – has a richness of meaning that is wider than simply an absence of conflict. It also has the positive sense of harmony or completeness, of each person finding and fitting in with their God-given role. Bishop John V Taylor described it as the harmony of a caring community that is inter-related and God-related.[5] *Shalom* includes the idea of 'space'. A church in the East End of London has reshaped its buildings not primarily for its own programmes, but to provide 'space' so that different local groups and networks can meet to discuss their concerns and hopes. During the week a wide variety of people meet on the premises – battered wives, political refugees, and those who are physically handicapped. In many deprived urban areas the local church is the only community able to provide such space.

There is not only the dimension of reconciliation or peace with God and the dimension of peace between people and communities. There is also the dimension of peace or restoration of right relationships between men and women and the environment. One of the Messianic passages in Isaiah describes how the 'wolf will lie with the lamb' (Is 11:6). The creation mandate to 'rule over . . . all the earth' (Gen 1:26) has sometimes been taken out of context and misused to justify the exploitation and destruction of the earth's resources. God's intention was that men and women would be responsible stewards of the environment, accountable to him.

Damage to the environment can be illustrated from the history of Israel and the promised land.[6] Because Israel refused to follow instructions to occupy the whole area intended for them the land became overcrowded; it was also devastated by a series of wars, many resulting from unwise or forbidden alliances. As a result the land flowing with milk and honey became barren, the tree cover disappeared and the soil was eroded away.

The Messianic promises of peace, however, include a vision of an environment restored – there are several passages in Isaiah which speak of 'streams in the desert' (Is 35:6), of the wilderness rejoicing and blossoming.

The Christian is called not only to find peace, but also to take the initiative to become a peacemaker (Mt 5:9). Michael Cassidy, director of the evangelistic organisation African Enterprise was frequently instrumental in bringing together political leaders from all sides in South Africa for a day of prayer – this was a significant factor behind the miraculous changes that later took place.

*Justice*

In the Messianic prophecies the ideal of peace is frequently linked with the themes of justice and righteousness. Peace at any price, or peace at the cost of allowing injustice to continue, is a false peace and cannot be a lasting one. A ruthless and oppressive regime may be accepted by the wealthy if it guarantees 'peace' from terrorism and guerrilla warfare, but the cost may be imprisonment without trial or the strange 'disappearance' of political opponents. Under the military dictatorship in Argentina 30,000 disappeared; many of them were dropped from aircraft into the Atlantic.

Christ was concerned for peace, but not at the expense of justice. His direct action to drive out the Temple traders who exploited the poor would probably be described by a policeman as 'a breach of the peace'. But it was ultimately for the sake of peace. Earlier on the Mount of Olives he had wept over the city of Jerusalem saying, 'If you . . . had only known . . . what would bring you peace' (Lk 19:42). One of the conditions of peace is repentance and a concern for justice.

There are some nurture programmes for new Christians that emphasise personal devotion and church attendance without including a social dimension and a concern for justice. One of the causes of this omission is the custom in some parts of the church of reading the Bible without taking note of its teaching on justice. The situation is not helped by some of our English translations. For example the Greek word *dikaiosune* appears frequently in the letter to the Romans, but is usually translated as 'righteousness' whereas it could also be translated as 'justice'. While 'righteousness' can and should be understood as having both a 'vertical' and 'horizontal' dimension it is not always read this way.

In using the word 'justice' it is important to note the distinction between 'justice' as equality before the law and justice in the sense of distributive justice. Equality before the law means that justice should be done 'without respect of persons'. Historically, Christianity has had a significant influence in preventing corruption and ensuring that all are treated equally before the law.

Justice in the distributive sense means that every citizen should have his or her 'basic necessities of life'. Every person needs a minimum standard of food, clothing and housing to maintain a human existence and dignity. It is in this connection that the term a 'just wage' is used. 'Distributive justice' may not necessarily mean equality as between one profession or job skill and another, but differences should not be disproportionate.

Raymond Fung, who for some years was the evangelism secretary of the World Council of Churches, has described distributive justice in terms of 'The Isaiah Agenda'. He argues that God wants communities in which:

> children do not die
> old people live in dignity
> people who build houses live in them; and
> those who plant vineyards eat fruit. (Is 65:20–23)[7]

## Liberation

In his first sermon at Nazareth (Lk 4:17 ff) Christ based the manifesto of his mission on the reading for the day which was one of the messianic prophecies in Isaiah (61:1–2):

> The Spirit of the Lord is on me
> because he has anointed me
> to preach good news to the poor.
> He has sent me to proclaim freedom for the prisoners
> and recovery of sight for the blind,
> to release the oppressed,
> to proclaim the year of the Lord's favour.

'Today,' he said, 'this scripture is fulfilled.' In saying this he was identifying himself with the figure of the servant portrayed in Isaiah, and identified the kingdom he came to inaugurate with the themes of liberation, peace and justice. Some have tried to spiritualise this passage by limiting it to liberation from personal sin and to insight for the spiritually blind. Others have interpreted it in a purely socio-political sense. However, it is clear from the ministry of Jesus and from the way he actually fulfilled this manifesto that he interpreted the work of liberation as relating to every dimension of life. Freedom from sin, for example, meant freedom from both personal sin and from corporate sin, as well as liberation for those suffering from the consequences of the sins of others.

The early Liberation Theologians in South America were fond of using the Exodus story as a description of the liberation that God brings. Exodus portrays a God who is concerned and gets involved – 'I have indeed seen the misery of my people . . . I am concerned about their suffering. So I have come down to rescue them . . .' (Ex 3:7–8). Clearly the God of Exodus is not a God of a spiritualised or privatised gospel; he is one who is concerned to bring hope of every kind in suffering. But nor is he a God who is concerned simply with freedom from political and economic oppression. The people of God were freed not only *from* oppression but also *for* the worship and service of God – 'When you have brought the people out of Egypt you will worship God on this mountain' (Ex 3:12).

Not only do the poor and oppressed need to be liberated but the rich need to be liberated as well, from the captivity and pressures of wealth. For the rich young ruler the cost of this liberation was too great, and as far as we know he never became a disciple (Lk 18:18 ff).

The connection between mission, evangelism and hope was made by the second Anglican-Roman Catholic International Commission:

> The source of the church's hope for the world is God, who has never abandoned the created order and has never ceased to work within it. It is called, empowered, and sent by God to proclaim this hope and to communicate to the world the conviction on which this hope is founded. Thus the church participates in Christ's mission to the world through the proclamation of the gospel of salvation by its words and deeds.[8]

## Unity and community

The principle of acceptance resulted in a Christian community in the early church that sought to transcend all divisions of race, class and gender. At one point this unity seems to have been pushed to the point of abolishing private property (Acts 2:44). Unity was considered to be a developing and maturing experience; the goal was for the community to mature into the likeness of Christ himself, with the characteristics of truth and love (Eph 4:15). It is no easy task to keep these characteristics in balance. Love without a concern for truth becomes mere sentiment, and love that is not built on the foundation of truth cannot last. Yet an orthodoxy that lacks love is 'a resounding gong or a clanging cymbal' (1 Cor 13:1).

The relationship of the different persons of the Trinity is both the *model* and the *source* of the unity and community that God wills for the church and for the world. The Christian understanding of the nature of God is that of one God in three persons – Father, Son and Holy Spirit – who relate to one another in a perfect harmony and unity. God did not need to create human beings in order to satisfy a need for relationships; our God is relational in his very being. From this it follows that Christians are intended to enter a relationship with the triune God and also with one another. This is made possible through the initiative of God in entering our lives. John records Jesus as saying, 'If anyone loves me, he will obey my teaching. My father will love him and we will come to him and make our home with him' (Jn 14:23). The presence of the Holy Spirit is also implied in this verse. It is as if the church, the people of God, becomes 'part of the extended divine family through the indwelling Spirit.'[9] As we turn to God we are caught up into the lasting relationship between the persons of the Trinity – we pray in the Spirit, through Christ to the Father (Rom 8:26).

The doctrine of the Trinity also provides a model of the balance between unity, community, equality and identity.[10] The 'persons' of the Trinity all have their own identity and diversity, but there is only one Godhead. Unity need not therefore mean uniformity, a flattening out of differences. Rather unity is a harmony of rich diversity. This has implications for church reunion schemes, but also for our vision of what a renewed society should be like. Nor does equality mean that everyone has to have the same function or that we should be so pre-occupied with 'rights' that we find it difficult to speak of 'duty', responsibility and sacrifice. The three persons of the Trinity are equal in essence but the Son and the Holy Spirit subordinate themselves in order to accomplish the Godhead's mission in the world. Both mission and unity are central to God's character. One of the key aims of mission and evangelism should be that of creating or restoring unity. On the other hand, one of the main motives for Christian unity should be for the sake of mission.

A good example of unity and community, with diversity, can be found in the Living Word Community in Philadelphia, USA. It is a multi-ethnic and bilingual church with Blacks, Anglos and Hispanics meeting together. All centralised activities apart from the Sunday morning worship service were cancelled and the life of the congregation was radically decentralised into small home meetings, where the tensions arising from racial and ethnic differences could be talked and worked through.[11]

Because we have a relational God every Christian is a relational being, but we could also say this of every person through creation. It is part of the nature of humanity to be relational. 'We learn from the doctrine of the blessed Trinity,' said C S Lewis, 'that something analogous to society exists within the divine being from all eternity.'[12] The ultimate goal, therefore, is not just the unity of all Christians but the unity of the whole of creation in Christ (Eph 1:10). The root meaning of the word 'ecumenism' relates not to the church but to the whole inhabited earth. As Bishop Desmond Tutu has put it, 'we need other human beings in order to be human.'[13]

The second Anglican-Roman Catholic International Commission declared:

> The will of God, Father, Son and Holy Spirit, is to reconcile to himself all that he has created and sustains, to set free the creation from its bondage to decay and to draw all humanity into communion with himself.[14]

## Transformation

An evangelist said to an enquirer, 'Christ is willing to accept you as you are but he won't let you stay as you are.' Talk of acceptance and liberation is inadequate unless we add transformation. It is the work of the Holy Spirit to remake us into the likeness of God (2 Cor 3:17–18).

Christians are not expected to be super-human, free from all weakness or suffering. Nor are we to be sub-human, insulated from normal human life, though the ghetto-like existence of some congregations can give this impression. The Spirit works within us to restore the image of God that has been marred by our rebellion and to make us as truly human as the Christ who is 'the Word made flesh'. We are to be filled with 'all the fullness of God' (Eph 3:19). We are to be his 'new people' (GNB) or new humanity.

A practical example of reconciliation and transformation can be found in the bridge-building encounter camps that were organised in South Africa by African Enterprise. Young people from the black, Indian and white communities would be invited. On one camp some black teenagers challenged the whites with the question, 'Do you know what you have done to us?' As they talked some of the tougher white teenagers were reduced to tears. As a sign of reconciliation young people from all three communities later walked down the street arm in arm.

The Spirit is at work not only to change individuals, but also society and the whole creation is described in the section below on hope. The later chapters of the letter to the Ephesians urge us to work out this transformation in the context of home and work.

## Salvation

The concepts of peace, justice, acceptance, liberation, unity and transformation can all be included in the word 'salvation'. The root word for salvation is *sozo*, a word that can mean to 'make whole'. It is often used in the gospels in connection with the healing of those who suffer. This subject will be discussed on pages 90–97. Salvation will be given fuller treatment in Chapter 3.

Strictly speaking there are three tenses to salvation. Those who put their trust in Christ have already been saved from the penalty of sin. Through the work of the Holy Spirit they are daily being saved from its power and one day they will be saved from its presence altogether. This is why 1 Pet 1:5 speaks of a salvation 'that is ready to be revealed in the last time'.

Although we have spoken in terms of individual believers it can be argued that salvation in the Old Testament is primarily a community concept.[15]

## Love

This is undoubtedly the foundational and most comprehensive gospel word. The others listed above in this chapter are all facets and dimensions of love and so this paragraph can be brief. Without love, however, peace, justice and community can be cold and unattractive. Love is the glow of the fire, the flow of the bloodstream, the sap that brings life to leaf and branch. One of the best known gospel verses is John 3:16 – 'God so loved the world that he gave his one and only Son.' When St Paul speaks of the gifts of justification, peace, access, joy and perseverance he crowns it all with the words, 'God has poured out his love into our hearts by the Holy Spirit' (Rom 5:1–5).

Disenchantment with materialism has led many to re-value relationships. The internationally famous pop singer Sting is reported as saying in February 1996, after being robbed of £6 million by his accountant, that it made him realise that his wealth was 'not in the bank . . . but in my friends, my family, my love of music.'[16]

## Life

God's gift of his Son is so 'that whoever believes in him shall not perish but have eternal life' (Jn 3:16). The adjective 'eternal' refers both to length and to quality. The gift offered is that of life that lasts beyond the grave, but also one that brings new dimensions to living now. A constant theme in the New Testament is that of being brought out of a state where we are alienated from the life of God, described as 'death', to the new life made available through the death and resurrection of Christ. This new life is described as being 'born anew' in the Spirit (Jn 3:3–6), and as 'knowing . . . God' (Jn 17:3). It is being caught up into the communal life of the Trinity both now and in the world to come.

Many of the qualities of this new life are linked with the other words in this chapter and especially that of love.

## Celebration and worship

In looking at the meaning of acceptance, we have seen how the idea of feasting and celebration is central to both Judaism and Christianity. There has sometimes been a debate as to whether worship or evangelism is the primary aim of the church. If pressed to decide it would be necessary to give ultimate priority of place to worship as this is an activity that continues into eternity, whereas evangelism does not. But the two are far more closely connected than is sometimes realised. Evangelism is linked to worship in that the primary purpose of mission and evangelism must be to glorify God and to bring others to worship him. One of the goals of Christian transformation is to make every part of daily life an offering of worship; our evangelism and even our suffering can be an offering to God. On the other hand worship can be both a motivation and a setting for evangelism. Worship that does not include or lead to the sharing of the glory of God with others has an important dimension missing. Witness has been defined as 'praise that is overheard'.

## Hope and eternity

Whether or not the human race avoids the catastrophes that could arise through the population explosion, pollution, destruction of the ozone layer or nuclear conflict[17] it seems likely that the universe as a whole is eventually heading for destruction. The predictions are that the end will be either a 'bang' or a 'whimper'. 'The history of the universe,' says John Polkinghorne, 'is a gigantic tug-of-war between the expansive force of the big bang, driving the galaxies apart, and the contractive force of gravity pulling them together.'[18] If expansion prevails, enormous black holes will appear and the world will end in a whimper. If gravity prevails the present expansion of the galaxies will be reversed and the whole world will collapse back into a 'single cosmic melting pot'. Although neither catastrophe is likely to happen for tens of billions of years, both possibilities raise the question as to whether the creation of the universe has been ultimately futile. However, cosmic death raises questions that are not dissimilar from those raised by human death. The issue of futility arises only if there is no ultimate future for the human race or for the universe. But the gospel hope is that God has a purpose for both. The whole creation is 'groaning as in the pain of childbirth' and 'will be liberated from its bondage to decay and brought into the glorious freedom of the children of God' (Rom 8: 21 and 22). It is as if suffering is the pathway to hope and transformation both for the individual and for creation.

The new creation that is promised will not be totally new in the sense of complete discontinuity with the present creation, but will be a transformation of it. Parallels can be drawn with the differences and similarities of the transformed body of Christ after the resurrection. His new body was similar, yet different, not always immediately recognised, yet discernible and freed from its earthly limitations. The victory won through the cross and resurrection over the forces of evil (Col 2:15) and over disease, decay and death will one day be complete. But the future hope for the creation and for those of the human race who do not choose to 'opt out' does not give us an excuse to sit back and wait for it to happen, rather it gives incentive to work for change in the assurance that one day complete transformation will be achieved. 'Thanks be to God! He gives us the victory through our Lord Jesus Christ. Therefore ... always give yourself fully to the work of the Lord, because you know that your labour in the Lord is not in vain' (1 Cor 15:57–58).

Issues from this chapter for discussion and action will be found on page 188.

## Notes

1. Professor David Ford and Alistair McFadyen, an essay entitled 'Praise' in 'God in the City' essays and reflections from the Archbishop of Canterbury's Urban Theology Group. Peter Sedgwick, ed. (Mowbray: London, 1995).

2. *The Measure of Mission* (Church House Publishing: London, 1987) p 38.

3. Paul Tillich, *Windows on Salvation*, ed. Donald English (Darton, Longman and Todd: London, 1994), p 53.

4. Simon Chan, a Pentecostal leader from Singapore, in his presentation to the 5th World Conference on Faith and Order, 'Sharing the Trinitarian Life' in *On the Way to Fuller Koinonia – the Official Report of the 5th World Conference on Faith and Order* (WCC Publications: Geneva, 1994), p 86.

5. J V Taylor, *Enough is Enough* (SCM: London, 1975) pp 41–42.

6. This is argued more fully by Professor Sam Berry in *Ecology and Ethics* (IVP: Leicester, 1972), p 21.

7. Raymond Fung, *The Isaiah Vision* (WCC: Geneva, 1992), p 5.

8. ARCIC Agreed Statement 1986, paragraph 31. Quoted in *Measure of Mission* (Church House Publishing: London, 1987), p 46.

9. Chan, *op cit*, p 87.

10. See for example *The Forgotten Trinity* a report of the

British Council of Churches Study Commission (BCC: London, 1989).

11. The story is told in *Transformation* magazine (Oxford, 5/4, 1988), pp 39–40

12. C S Lewis, *The Problem of Pain* (Fount: London, 1978), p 17.

13. Quoted in *On the Way To Fuller Koinonia – the Official Report of the 5th World Conference on Faith And Order* (WCC Publications: Geneva, 1994), p 99.

14. ARCIC II, *Salvation and the Church* (Anglican Consultative Council: 1987), p 9.

15. This is argued by Bishop John B Taylor in *Windows on Salvation* ed. Donald English, op cit, p 12.

16. Reported in an interview with Miranda Sawyer and published in *The Observer* supplement, February 1996.

17. Described in Chapter 1.

18. John Polkinghorne, *Science and Christian Belief* (SPCK: London, 1994) p 162.

# CHAPTER THREE

# PIE IN THE SKY?

*Evangelism with a Social Dimension*

The Introduction began with the story of a missionary throwing a copy of St John's Gospel through his car window to a man by the roadside. The story illustrates an understanding of evangelism that is one end of an extreme. It implies a number of assumptions. The first is that the 'spiritual' welfare of a person is so important that social needs are secondary and in practice do not need to be taken into account by the evangelist. The individual is 'a soul to be saved' rather than a person to be helped. One popular way of describing this approach is 'pie in the sky when you die', rather than 'hope on the ground while you're still around'.

The second assumption is that social problems are the result of personal sin. This may of course be true in specific instances. Alcoholism can lead to loss of work, family and home, though there may be social causes to the alcoholism in the first place. But this extreme attitude assumes that all social problems are the result of depravity rather than deprivation or both.

The third assumption follows logically; it is that social evils are not to be remedied by social reform but by evangelism in the narrow sense of bringing about individual conversions. The argument is that once a significant percentage of the population become committed Christians, social reform will take place automatically.

Again there is some truth in this. Significant social change took place as a result of John Wesley's evangelism, but it can be shown that his work had a strong social dimension and it is doubtful from history whether social change will normally take place as a result of a 'privatised' evangelism which lacks a social dimension. It is significant that privatised evangelism has been popular among many white South Africans and among many Protestants in Northern Ireland and in the South of the USA. In many parts of the United States over 40% of the population go to church, but the state of society is not noticeably more moral or just than in other countries.

The historical roots of 'privatised evangelism' can be found in the United States in the period following the Civil War. It was a period when 'premillennial' theology was in the ascendant. This theology takes literally the prophecy in the book of Revelation (Chapter 20) that Christ will return and will reign with his saints for a thousand years. It is 'premillennial' in the sense that Christ is expected to return prior to this thousand year era of peace and justice. Until he returns the world will go from worse to worse. The extreme premillennialist will therefore argue that until this happens it is irrelevant to have a social or political agenda. The best that can be hoped for is to contain some of the evil and to wait until all wrongs are righted during the millennium.

The great North American evangelist D L Moody illustrates this school of thought. He started one of his sermons with the words, 'I looked upon this world as a wrecked vessel. God has given me a lifeboat and said to me, "Moody; save all you can!"'[1] Those who became Christians through Moody's widespread ministry in the United States and in Britain were therefore discouraged from social or political involvement. The world was doomed and the only course for the Christian therefore was to escape from the world. While compassionate action such as Christian medical work was encouraged, action to bring about lasting social change was likened to a householder rearranging the furniture when the house is on fire, or to a crew member rearranging the deckchairs on the *Titanic*.

But as we have seen Christians have a calling to become involved in promoting peace, justice and social change. A more appropriate nautical analogy therefore is to compare the world to a vessel which has been taken over by pirates; the task is to regain control and so save the ship.

Premillennial teaching and in particular lifeboat theology have crossed the Atlantic. Even in the 1970s a leading minister could say, 'Military dictatorships are good for the gospel.' What he meant was that evangelism and missionary work in general were less likely to be interrupted by insurgents and by terrorist activity when there was strong government control. The phrase implies, however, that the gospel relates solely to a 'spiritual' realm and has nothing to say about human rights and just economies. The gospel is not neutral about dictatorships and other forms of government; it cannot be said or should not be said that the gospel is being spread if the result is simply church growth and not justice, peace and the protection of human rights. It is in the interests of dictators of the left or right to have churches that preach a 'spiritual' or 'privatised' gospel which can divert attention from social injustice. Such a gospel can become an 'opiate of the masses'.[2] 'Pie in the sky when you die' becomes attractive when there is little hope on the ground. Those who preach a comprehensive gospel which addresses social as well as personal and family issues are not always treated favourably. In the 1980s many outspoken Roman Catholic priests in South America were imprisoned, tortured and even killed. A much publicised case was that of Archbishop Oscar Romero who was shot in March 1980 while preaching during a Mass in El Salvador.

The 'Moody' or 'Lifeboat' gospel on the other hand has affinities with the teaching of the Pharisees. They dehumanised the law by making the duty to love God independent of the duty to love our neighbours. For the Pharisee 'righteousness' and 'right religion' could be considered quite apart from the social context in which the worshipper was set. So long as God's sabbath was religiously observed it did not matter if a sufferer was denied healing on that day.[3] In Matthew chapter 23 Jesus accuses the Pharisees of keeping the minutiae of the law, but neglecting the more important matters of justice, mercy and faithfulness (Mt 23:23). Externally they were scrupulous in external ceremonial cleansing, but inwardly they were full of greed and self-indulgence. Jesus however is concerned for a holistic (or whole) lifestyle that is holy in every dimension.

In his book *Liberal Evangelism* Bishop John Saxbee describes a visit made in 1988 to the country of Rwanda. He felt that the gospel being preached failed to relate to the social context and sensed that he had more personal affinity to Peace Corps volunteers than to missionaries. If his comments are valid they may go some way towards explaining how a country renowned for the 'East African Revival' experienced such violent conflict in the 1990s. His view is endorsed by the Rev Roger Bowen, Secretary of Mid Africa Ministries, formerly the Rwanda Mission: he argues that the pietist tradition of the missionaries in the area was reinforced in the Anglican Church by the use of the premillennialist Schofield Bible. Schofield was recorded as saying at a conference in 1914, 'There is no hope for humanity except in the personal return of the Lord of glory.'[4] The lessons from Rwanda can be paralleled, for example, from some early missionary work in China, where a truncated 'privatised' gospel was also preached. In 1877 Matthew Arnold described the Church of England as 'an institution devoted above all to the landed gentry, but also to the propertied and satisfied classes generally; favouring immobility, preaching submission and reserving transformation in general for the other side of the grave.'

## The social gospel

The other-worldly 'lifeboat theology' can be matched at the other end of the spectrum by the 'social gospel'. There is a proper use of the term 'social gospel', when the phrase is intended to mean a gospel that relates to the whole of life, but historically it is frequently used to describe a gospel that is almost entirely socio-political and 'this worldly'. This is the usage being employed in this chapter.

There have been times when some of the pronouncements of the World Council of Churches have seemed to be at this extreme. At the WCC Assembly at Bangkok in 1973 it was said that 'Salvation is the peace of the people in Vietnam, independence in Angola and justice and reconciliation in Northern Ireland.'[5] While the fruits of salvation, or even salvation itself might be said to include these things salvation is not just reconciliation between countries and peoples. Men and women need to be reconciled to God as individuals and have their lives transformed by receiving the Spirit of Christ. When this happens they are given new motivation, strength and hope. This can be illustrated by the case of a small congregation on a housing estate in Liverpool which started lobbying the local council to meet some of the social needs on the estate. They joined in partnership with others outside the church in order to promote change, but progress was slow and difficult and most of the others gave up the struggle. The members of the congregation were, however, able to keep going and said, 'It is our faith that made us stick.'

The WCC may not have intended to exclude other dimensions of salvation such as the conversion of individuals and their personal faith in Christ in the Bangkok definition, but many involved in the Lausanne movement (described below), such as Dr John Stott, found this concept of salvation a cause for concern. It seems to merit Niebuhr's famous critique of the one dimensional 'social gospel':

A God without wrath brought men without sin into a kingdom without judgment through the ministrations of a Christ without a cross.[6]

*Evangelism as a partner of social action*

D L Moody and the Bangkok statement are at two opposite ends of a spectrum. There are many positions in between. Missions in the nineteenth century and the first part of the twentieth would very often have a social programme, though this tended to focus on schools and hospitals rather than developing business, industry or trade[7] and still less on challenging the socio-political structures. But there were exceptions as, for example, when missionaries came into conflict with the East India Company.

One position on the spectrum is that represented by the evangelical 'Lausanne movement'[8] which began with a conference at Lausanne in Switzerland in 1974. The Lausanne Covenant drawn up at the end of the conference stated that 'evangelism and social-political involvement are both part of our Christian duty' though it argued that 'evangelism is primary'.

More recent times have seen something of a convergence between the WCC and its earlier critics, especially the Lausanne Movement. In 1982 the WCC Central Committee approved a report drawn up by the Commission on World Mission and Evangelism entitled 'Mission and Evangelism: an Ecumenical Statement'. The report commented that:

Sin, alienating persons from God, neighbour and nature, is found both in individual and corporate forms, both in slavery of the human will and in social, political and economic structures of domination and dependence. The church is sent into the world to call people and nations to repentance, to announce forgiveness of sin and a new beginning in relations with God and with neighbours through Jesus Christ.[9]

This statement is clearly intended to bring together the personal and the socio-political elements of the gospel. 'Privatised evangelism' had almost exclusively focused on individual and personal sin, while the 'social gospel' had focused on sin to be found in social structures, multi-national companies and governments.

The Lausanne Covenant had stated that 'evangelism and social-political involvement are both part of our Christian duty', but further work was needed to spell out the relationship between the two. A 'Lausanne' Consultation on the Relationship between Evangelism and Social Responsibility (CRESR) was held in 1980 and its report argued that there were three possible relationships in practice. First social concern or action could be the *fruit* of evangelism.[10] Once an individual or a community had accepted the gospel they would or could be motivated to social concern as one of the fruits of evangelism. One example of this can be found among the Indian communities of Northern Argentina. Although the early evangelism had been accompanied by educational and medical work significant programmes of social change came later and included a project to protect the Indians' traditional lands. The link was expressed this way: 'They have a stronghold in heaven so it is only right that they should have a foothold on earth.'

The consultation also noted that engagement in a social project might give opportunity for witness – here social action is the *prelude* to evangelism. Finally evangelism and social action might *partner* each other, social action and witness taking place at the same time. An example of this from Hong Kong is given on page 66.

The report used the analogy of scissors where the two aspects of mission – evangelism and social action – are the two blades that need to cut together. However evangelism was still regarded as primary.

The consultation's approach can nevertheless still be criticised as falling into the danger of 'dualism'. If evangelism is a separate activity distinguished from social action and if it is primary, evangelists can still justify programmes that omit social concern. It is healthier to see evangelism and social action as overlapping dimensions of mission (see Figure 3 on page 16). Those engaged in social action should normally let it be known, either explicitly or implicity, that their work is done in the name and in the strength of Christ. One example of this is the work of Mother Teresa. There are, however, occasions where this may not be possible or appropriate, as in certain Islamic countries. On the other hand, those evangelising should have a social dimension to their work and message, as I will illustrate.

The Church of England Report 'Living Faith in the City' described the dangers of the two extremes; on the one hand there is a danger of 'a sectarian church, concerned only with spiritualised personal and individual salvation'. This 'cannot be a symbol of incarnation'. On the other hand there is the danger of 'a politicised church, ideologically committed to human progress only through human struggle'. This leaves no room for the intervention of the grace of God.[11]

## *'Holistic or integral evangelism'*

This is where social action and evangelism are each a dimension of the other. A New Testament illustration comes from Luke's report on the conversion of Zacchaeus (Lk 19). Tax collectors were unpopular, being seen as collaborators with the Roman government, and were usually guilty of lining their pockets by charging more tax than was required. It was therefore a courageous and merciful action on the part of Jesus to associate with such an unpopular and immoral person. In the middle of the crowd Jesus stopped by the sycamore tree which Zacchaeus had climbed and publically said, 'Come down immediately. I must stay at your house today' (Lk 19:5). Jesus' approach is one of acceptance even before Zacchaeus repents, but when repentance comes it has a social and economic dimension; the tax collector offers to give half his goods to the poor and to repay four-fold those he had cheated. There must have been a long queue outside the tax office later that day.

Several modern illustrations of integral evangelism are given by Raymond Fung in his book *The Isaiah Vision*. Raymond Fung was formerly secretary for evangelism of the World Council of Churches and later became senior secretary of the Hong Kong Christian Institute. He tells the story of two young Christian women who were textile workers in Hong Kong. One Christmas they invited some of the other workers to join them in a Bible study. They read Luke's story of how Mary in pregnancy had to travel a long distance and they were struck by the risk this must have meant for her health and the life of her baby. They linked it with current Hong Kong labour legislation; this provided for maternity leave, but the leave was offered without pay and no working-class woman could afford to claim it. The Christian women joined with others in fighting for a change in the law. It was a costly and a lengthy struggle but it ended in victory and during the struggle a number of women became Christians.[12]

The phrase 'integral evangelism' holds together 'the fanning of faith and the promoting of justice as twin gospel imperatives'.[13] This is a balance that we need to hold primarily as a matter of principle, but also because without it our evangelism will often be ineffective. If we are blind to the suffering of others they will be deaf to the gospel.

This 'whole' or 'holistic' attitude to life is common in many two-thirds world cultures, which do not make the separation common to Western secularised societies. Indian pastors in Northern Argentina had difficulty in understanding why large sums of money were available from Christian relief and development agencies for clinics, but not for churches. 'Don't you Christians in the first world see worship as important?' they asked. Emphasising either the material without the spiritual or vice versa is a division that is strange both to modern two-thirds world cultures and to the Bible.

*An integral evangelism diagram*

Walter Wink has a valuable series of diagrams to illustrate different world-views.[14]

1. The **spiritualistic world-view** divides human beings into 'soul' and 'body'. Matter is either indifferent or downright evil. In Figure 6 there is therefore a break line between heaven and earth and a cross through the lower circle. This world-view is usually associated with Gnosticism, but could be associated with 'privatised evangelism', where the church is not much more than a departure lounge where people await their flight call to the sky.

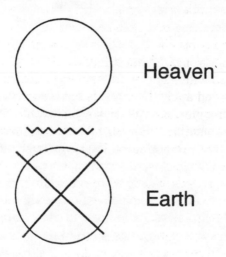

*Figure 6: The spiritualistic world-view*

2. The **materialistic world-view** believes there is nothing but material existence. It became prominent in the Enlightenment, but there are times when some sections of the church speak and live as if they hold to this view. Just as 'practical atheists' may not deny God's existence but live without reference to him, so there are those who live as if God does not in practice intervene. In Figure 7 there is again a break line between heaven and earth, but this time the cross comes through the heaven circle.

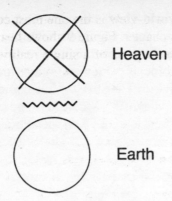

*Figure 7: The materialistic world-view*

3. The **theological world-view** is so called because it represents the thinking of a number of Christian theologians, preserves a supernatural realm, but makes it hermetically sealed and immune to challenge from the sciences. Figure 8 has no break line between heaven and earth, but nor does it have a connecting line. The materialistic world-view believes that the spiritual world is an illusion; the theological world-view preserves a privileged 'spiritual' realm immune to confirmation or refutation. In that respect apologetics is irrelevant.

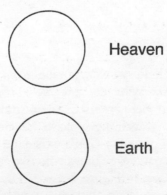

*Figure 8: The theological world-view*

4. The **integral world-view** is the one most consistent with the argument of this chapter. Figure 9 shows heaven and earth as the inner and outer aspects of a single reality – integrated, rather than separated.

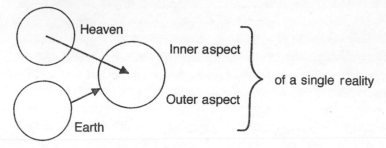

*Figure 9*

## The work of the Messiah

We can only have a fully-rounded biblical understanding of evangelism if we recognise that the gospel does not break in as something totally new with the New Testament; it is the fulfilment of Old Testament promises and hopes. The Messiah or the Christ is portrayed in Isaiah as a servant who is concerned for justice:

> Here is my servant whom I uphold . . . I will put my Spirit upon him and he will bring justice to the nations . . . I will . . . make you . . . a light to the Gentiles, to open eyes that are blind, to free captives from prison and to release from the dungeon those who sit in darkness (Is 42:1–7).

A similar theme comes several chapters later where the servant is said to 'preach good news to the poor', to 'bind up the broken hearted, to proclaim freedom for the captives and release for the prisoners' (Is 61:1–2). The phrase 'preach good news' in these verses has as its equivalent in the Greek translation of the Old Testament[15] the verb *euangellizo*, to 'evangelise'.

Is this then the Old Testament understanding of evangelism? We saw in Chapter 2 the significance of the fact that when Jesus entered the synagogue at Nazareth at the beginning of his ministry he opened the scroll to read this passage (Is 61) and declared 'Today this scripture is fulfilled in your hearing' (Lk 4:16–21). In so doing he was claiming to be the servant Christ or Messiah and to fulfil in his person the role of the servant set out in Isaiah. Preaching 'good news to the poor' and 'releasing the oppressed' were therefore part of the manifesto of his programme. It has already been noted that this passage has been interpreted in different ways. Privatised evangelists have argued that Christ's programme is to bring recovery of spiritual sight and release for those made captive by sin. The 'social gospel' interprets this passage almost entirely in social and political terms. In fact both the 'spiritual' and personal, and also the social and political, are valid dimensions.

Bishop Lesslie Newbigin has summarised the social dimension of evangelism well: 'Conversion is not a transference from one self-centred community to another; it is not a private peace with God while the whole world goes to rot. It is being caught up into God's action of kingdom. It is being changed so that we can be agents of change.'[16]

It is sometimes argued by the exponents of a privatised gospel that Jesus avoided conflict with the government of his day and did not confront the Roman authorities on social and political issues. We have to remember, however, that in a number of areas the 'ecclesiastical' authorities had social and political power. Jesus was quite prepared to be confrontational over the needs of the poor and the way they were oppressed by legalistic interpretations of the law. He was revolutionary concerning the position of women, the use of political power, the possession of wealth and the observance of the sabbath. It was on these grounds, as well as on the charge of blasphemy, that he was eventually arrested. Significantly one of the charges against him was that of treason – it was a trumped-up charge but it would have had no credibility if his programme had been totally 'other-worldly'.

The ministry of Jesus was not limited to the spiritual realm. He was the Word made flesh (Jn 1:14). In him the good news was embodied or incarnated – it was not simply a disembodied message or voice from heaven.

Nor is the 'hope' for the future that the gospel presents a solely 'spiritual' one. The Christian does not become a disembodied spirit after death, but is given a resurrection body. Even the creation itself 'will be liberated from its bondage to decay' (Rom 8:21). The good news is therefore about reconciliation and transformation as between God and his children, between one person and another, between one nation or community and another, and between humankind and the environment. This transformation takes place through a process of suffering or struggle.

## Jesus and the kingdom

The social dimension of the gospel is also illustrated by the frequent references to the kingdom of God or heaven in the first three gospels. The first recorded message of Jesus according to Mark is described in these words: 'After John was put in prison, Jesus went into Galilee, proclaiming the good news of God. "The time has come," he said. "The kingdom of God is near. Repent and believe the good news!"' (Mk 1:14–15).

There is a sense in which God's kingdom is thought of as arriving with the coming of Jesus, but there is another sense in which it is 'now and not yet'. God's kingdom will not be fully seen or established until the end of time – that is why we pray in the Lord's Prayer 'your kingdom come' (Mt 6:10). It may help to avoid the idea that the kingdom is a place or a particular territory if we use a phrase like 'God's reign' rather than 'kingdom'. When we become a disciple of Christ we submit to

God's reign, but that reign has to penetrate to every part of our lives, and to every part of society. To understand and to submit more fully to God's reign takes a lifetime of discipleship.

Privatised evangelism tends not to use kingdom language or at least fails to recognise its social and political implications. On the other hand 'social gospel' theologians need to be reminded that it is inconsistent to speak of welcoming the kingdom without being ready to encounter and submit to the king. The promise of the kingdom is one that gives hope in our chaotic and disturbed world.

One of the significant factors in the collapse of communism, especially in Romania, was the witness of the church. The revolution started when the police came to arrest an outspoken pastor, Lazlo Tokes, and crowds of protesters blocked the way to his house forming a human barrier. His comment when he visited the WCC Central Committee in March 1990 was, 'I think it is no coincidence that the revolution began at the Reformed church at Temesvar . . . God wants to use his churches for the renewal of society.'

## The Great Commission

Similarly 'the Great Commission' in Matthew 28: 18–20 refers not only to personal commitment to Christ and to church growth but also to the promotion of the kingdom values of justice and peace. This is only evident as a result of careful reading, and many church growth commentators simply relate the phrases 'go and make disciples of all nations, baptising them . . . and teaching them to obey everything I have commanded you . . .' to personal commitment and church growth. The late South African missiologist David Bosch argued that the Great Commission was a summary of the teaching of Matthew's gospel, whether by Matthew as he believed or added at a later date by the early church. It must therefore be understood in the light of the first gospel as a whole. The disciples we make must be disciples of Christ and his kingdom and the teaching that we give must include the kingdom values spelt out in the Sermon on the Mount (Chapters 5 to 7) and elsewhere.[17] As Dr William Abraham has put it, 'The responsible evangelist will be concerned to win as many converts as possible, but to win them is not just to get them to sign up but to introduce them in a realistic and honest fashion to the reign of God.'[18]

Too often the church has taken on board the individualistic culture of modern Western society. The gospel is often presented in terms of 'What can Jesus do for me?' Normally evangelistic booklets focus on the individual and his or her needs of identity, value and forgiveness. Reference to community involvement and responsibility is brief, comes later and is mainly related to the church rather than to the world. But the Bible begins with the community and then goes on to the individual's place within it. Our evangelistic booklets should focus on God's plan for society and for the world and then go on to the individual's place within that plan.

This emphasis should be demonstrated more clearly in the churches' rites of initiation such as baptism and confirmation. As Archbishop David Hope has put it, 'It is reasonable to suppose that the laying on of hands associated with Christian initiation was intended to symbolise both ordination to the ministerial priesthood of the laity and also coronation in the kingly office of those appointed to share the kingship of Christ.'[19] If we are called to share in the kingship of Christ we have the responsibility, authority and power to work for the extension of his kingdom.

Sometimes those who begin with a limited gospel which relates almost entirely to an individual's spiritual and religious needs have their thinking broadened by exposure to a different context. Several years ago my wife and I moved from suburbia to an inner-city vicarage. Soon after we arrived the door bell rang and the woman who stood there asked, 'Can I come in to talk about a problem I am facing?' I invited her in and at the back of my mind was the assumption that this might be an opportunity for a 'spiritual' chat ending up with the gift of an evangelistic booklet. But it turned out that she was about to be taken to court by her landlord who wanted to evict her in order to sell his property. A talk with the landlord, who lived in the flat above, revealed that he himself was a victim of the property market which had been distorted by rich newcomers moving into the area. It was impossible to find a quick solution to that particular woman's problem as she had left the visit to the vicarage as a last resort and it was now too late. But it did lead to a consideration of housing problems in general and to the founding of a church housing organisation.

*Evangelism, evangelisation and the transformation of structures*

Some confusion arose in 1990 because the Pope had called for a 'Decade of Evangelisation' while the Church of England, and Anglican Bishops worldwide, had called for a 'Decade of Evangelism'. The two words could be interpreted as having virtually the same meaning. In practice, however, the word evangelism tends to be used in a more focused sense of announcing or sharing the gospel and inviting people to become disciples of Christ. 'Evangelisation' is used more widely. The papal document *Evangelii Nuntiandi* declared that 'evangelising means bringing the good news into all the strata of humanity and through its influence transforming humanity from within and making it new'. However paragraph 36 makes it clear that personal transformation is essential as well. 'Structures which are more human and just must be built up, but the church recognises that even the best systems become inhuman if those who live in them do not undergo a conversion of heart and outlook.'[20]

The document rightly emphasises the need to change structures and not just to bring temporary relief to social problems. It is no good repairing the road if it goes in the wrong direction.[21] Some years ago Christian Aid used the illustration of an imaginary factory which had dangerous machinery; as a result a large number of workers suffered injury. The local churches set up a First Aid post at the factory gates so that workers could be treated and bandaged up, but when they went back into work they were injured again. Christian Aid likened the factory machinery to international trade structures that benefited the first world, but injured the economies of the two-thirds world. There are several cases where there has been increased production of goods such as coffee, but the income to the country concerned has not increased because the prices fixed by the trade structures have fallen. What is needed is not just 'first aid' but a change of structures.

Waldron Scott, president of Holistic Ministries International, is based in Paterson, New Jersey, in the United States. He and his wife, Georgia, founded a programme under the title 'Leadership Paterson' for equipping citizens in civic engagement and expanded the much-used fishing analogy:

If you give a man a fish you feed him for a day;
but if you train him how to fish you feed him for a lifetime.

They added, 'It does not help a man to fish if he is denied access to the stream; and it may even kill him if the stream is polluted. We are trying to work simultaneously on all four levels: charity, training, access and accountability.'[22]

An example of concern for the environment can be found in the rural parish of Stanton-by-Derby, in England. It has met the social needs of the village by providing a village shop and post office when the old one closed down – these are essential focal points for community life. It has also bought up part of a local wood and declared it a conservation area. Many other rural churches have set apart sections of their churchyards as conservation areas.

As we saw in the Introduction there is a sense in which we are free to use words in any way we like. However it has been made clear in this chapter that it can be dangerous to define evangelism in a narrow sense, to relate it solely to a religious or spiritual dimension and to separate it from social concern. This was the trap that some Christians and churches fell into in Nazi Germany. Furthermore those who claim that they separate evangelism from social concern do not always do so in practice, especially when they gain the advantage. Archbishop Desmond Tutu has frequently commented as follows on the early white settlers in South Africa, 'Before they arrived we had the land and they had the Bible; after they came we had the Bible, but they had the land.' In other cases a failure to relate the gospel to socio-political concerns may imply that there is no problem with the status quo, but this in itself is a socio-political statement. Such an assumption is implied by the third verse of the hymn *All Things Bright and Beautiful*, 'The rich man in his castle, the poor man at his gate . . . God ordered their estate.' The verse implies that if the state of the poor is so ordered, it is inappropriate to seek to change it.

We have spoken of integral evangelism as holding together 'the fanning of faith and the promoting of justice as twin gospel imperatives' (page 66). A common definition of evangelism is that of 'awakening personal faith';[23] undoubtedly this should be central to any definition of evangelism, but on its own it is dangerously open to the distortion of privatised evangelism, even though some who use this definition maintain that evangelism should always be set in the context of other dimensions of mission. A safer definition is the one used in the Introduction on page 15:

**'Sharing the good news of Jesus Christ, together with his invitation to become his disciples, and to join with him in his work of transforming the world.'**

In the Introduction (page 16) we illustrated integral evangelism with a set of overlapping circles, where evangelism is the announcing/inviting element that relates to worship, discipling, fellowship and social action as in Figure 10.

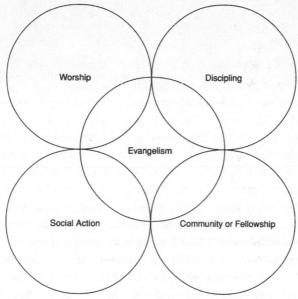

*Figure 10*

An excellent and more comprehensive, but lengthy definition was given by the late David Bosch in his work *Transforming Mission*:

'. . . that dimension and activity of the church's mission which by word and deed and in the light of particular conditions and a particular context, offers every person and community everywhere a valid opportunity to be directly challenged to a radical orientation of their lives, a reorientation which involves such things as a deliverance from slavery to the world and its powers; embracing Christ as Saviour and Lord; becoming a living member of his community the church; being enlisted into his service of reconciliation, peace and justice on earth; and being committed to God's purpose of placing all things under the rule of Christ.'[24]

## The implications of integral evangelism

Integral evangelism includes not only a personal and religious dimension, but also a social and political one. The following sections give theological and practical illustrations of the ways integral evangelism affects such issues as how the character of God and the nature of discipleship are presented. Some of the most important implications are for evangelists themselves.

### The evangelist

Some evangelists claim that their gifts and calling are primarily to evangelise in the narrower sense of bringing individuals to faith and incorporating them into the church. Although such evangelists seek to work on the frontiers of the church and the world, their ministry could probably be described as primarily church-focused rather than world-focused. The different members of Christ's body have a variety of gifts – some are described as primarily being for the building up of the body of Christ (as in Eph 4:11). The gifts listed in Romans 12, however, could be for the church or for the world or both as they include service, encouragement, leadership and mercy. It is quite proper, therefore, that some members of the church should exercise gifts and a calling that is partly or primarily focused on ministry within the church, while others may be called to give a good deal of their time to work in the community. A local Councillor, for example, would quite rightly not have the same amount of time for ministry within the church.

The evangelist may also claim that he or she (it is usually he) does not have the expertise to pronounce on social or political issues and that this task should be left to those who have that expertise. To some extent this is valid. It is one thing to identify a social problem and to challenge those in power to bring about change. It is another to recommend a detailed solution, especially where the choices of solution are along party-political lines and where Christians are divided as to the best way forward. On the other hand, if evangelists fail to have an adequate social and political dimension to their ministry and message then the good news is distorted.

Sometimes evangelists are faced with a practical dilemma where they cannot avoid taking a stance which has socio-political implications. An extreme example occurred on several occasions under the apartheid laws in the old South Africa. Should evangelistic meetings be open to all, both black and white together? If this were practically impossible should they go ahead, with different meetings for white and black? When mixed meetings did take place this made an important statement.

There were similar tensions facing missionaries working under the old Latin-American dictatorships. Should evangelistic campaigns address issues of oppression? If they didn't then the good news was distorted. If they did the campaigns might be stopped. There were particular difficulties for expatriate personnel. If they spoke out there would be the added complication of a foreigner criticising the local government and the fact that while they might only be risking the loss of a visa and expulsion, local Christians might be risking imprisonment and torture.

In one case a group of expatriate personnel decided that the way forward was to prepare a series of Bible studies on Amos for the use of local church members. As local Christians met together to study Amos they were helped to see the general principles of God's justice, but they also began to draw their own specific applications to the local scene. It was important that they, rather than the expatriate personnel, did this.

*The character of God*

Perhaps the most important question is to ask what sort of God is being presented by the evangelist? Is he a God who seems to be concerned only with personal 'spiritual' issues, or is he, as described on page 49 the God of Exodus who is also concerned with social issues? If there had not been the Bible studies on Amos described above a distorted picture of the character of God might have emerged.

## *The scope of sin and repentance*

Integral evangelism will make reference to corporate as well as to individual sin, and repentance will have a social dimension as we saw with Zacchaeus. It is significant that the repentance called for by John the Baptist had a social dimension. Soldiers and tax collectors were challenged to give up extortion and fraud and those with two coats were to give one away (Lk 3:7–14).

Some evangelists have in the past focused simply on what can be described as 'micro-ethics', applying the challenge of the gospel in terms of exhortations to regular church attendance, Bible reading, prayer and abstinence from alcohol and tobacco, but not referring to the major issues of social justice. However sin is not a disease that is located simply in individuals; it permeates systems and structures.

On the other hand the ideal of bringing the gospel challenge of repentance to structural as well as to individual sin is often far from easy in practice. People are sometimes powerless, or feel powerless, to take action. Nor is it easy for church leaders to free themselves from the everyday running of the church in order to help those facing major ethical issues. A senior business executive complained that on one occasion when the local minister called he was facing an extremely critical decision in his business over whether he should take action that would result in thousands of workers in India becoming redundant. He would have liked to discuss it with the minister, but the latter simply asked to see the executive's wife in order to finalise the Women's Meeting programme. Maybe the minister would not have been equipped to come up with answers, and probably the businessman should have taken the initiative in sharing the problem, but too often we can give the impression that we have neither the time nor the inclination to relate gospel principles to major social issues.

These decisions are not easy ones and churches do not often provide the kind of support needed.

## The nature of discipleship

The German Christian, Dietrich Bonhoeffer, who was martyred for his condemnation of the Nazi regime, used to warn of the dangers of what he called 'cheap grace'. By that he meant a style of evangelism that offered salvation at minimum cost to the would-be disciple. This was certainly not Jesus' approach; he challenged the rich young ruler to give up his wealth and called all those who wanted to follow him to be ready to 'take up the cross'.

Some evangelistic messages so focus on the meeting of personal needs – release from loneliness, peace of mind, a purpose in life – that the impression is given that the convert can 'take on' discipleship like an (eternal) life insurance policy without any radical change of lifestyle. But the task of evangelism should be one of 'enlisting people for the reign of God'. It is a call to a life of 'openness, vulnerability, wholeness and love'.[25] Jim Wallis has described conversion as 'the beginning of active solidarity with the purposes of the kingdom of God'.[26]

The implications of discipleship would of course have been much clearer in New Testament times; many of those called literally 'left everything' to follow Christ and to share in his ministry and mission. Yet even today self-denial, risk and vulnerability may be unavoidable for many who follow Christ.

When does the Christian stay in an imperfect or even corrupt structure in order to influence it from within and when does she or he come out? A committed Christian stance can be costly. As one businessman put it, 'Every day I go into work I know it may be my last.' His integrity prevented him from giving a dishonest presentation to prospective clients, and there was therefore the constant danger that the profits made in his section would as a result fall below average. The consequences could be loss of promotion or even redundancy. He had come to the point, however, where he was prepared to leave the issue in the hands of God, and to go into the office recognising that each day could be the last in that or any job.

There is, of course, a need for balance. A good deal of evangelistic ministry in the early church and today properly includes the meeting of individual needs and very often those needs will be the initial contact point. We shall see this particularly in what is said about healing below (pages 89 to 96). The challenge to discipleship should not give the impression that our acceptance by Christ is a reward for dedication and sacrifice rather than an undeserved gift of grace. Furthermore the implications of discipleship are sometimes revealed a step at a time. It is doubtful whether the apostles foresaw all the challenges ahead of them when they first began to follow Christ.

However, an evangelism that suggests a gospel of meeting individual needs without presenting the challenge of the kingdom is guilty of offering 'cheap grace'. The Rev Roger Bowen, commenting on the tragic events in Rwanda in 1995, has argued that the church there was strong on winning converts but weak on making disciples.

> There would be many calls in preaching to repent and believe the gospel but little teaching on how to live out Christian discipleship in the secular world and how to be salt and light in society . . . it is a sharp reminder that mere growth in numbers, without a quality of costly discipleship, is empty and powerless to confront the pressures of evil.

He also comments that 'the church has operated with a very privatised and inadequate view of sin'.[27] Parallels can be found in Britain and John Wimber comments that in the United States 'a cheap-grace gospel is frequently preached, producing weak

Christians who do not stand when powerful and persuasive attacks come from the world'.[28]

## The breadth of salvation

A word that is frequently linked with conversion is 'salvation'. Some years ago a Salvation Army worker found herself sitting opposite a Bishop in a train and said to him, 'Are you saved?' His reply was, 'It depends what you mean; I have been saved, I am being saved, and I will be saved.' As described in Chapter 2 (page 53) the New Testament has three tenses of salvation. The past tense is referred by some to the moment of baptism, or conversion; by some it is referred back 2,000 years to the crucifixion and resurrection of Christ, when our salvation was secured. However the work of the Holy Spirit in freeing and rescuing us from self-centredness and sin is a process that continues in the present. Then we look forward to the day at the end of time when we are fully liberated and are revealed as children of God (Rom 8:19).

Salvation has a social dimension. The word 'save' (*sozo*) is used in a number of 'physical' ways. It is often used in the context of healing; a blind man healed at the entrance to Jericho is told, 'Thy faith hath saved thee' (Lk 18:42 AV). The New International Version translates *sozo* here as 'healed'. The word is also used in the story of the storm on the lake 'Lord, save us' (Mt 8:25). Zacchaeus' repentance included a restoration of wrongs. It is interesting to note that he was *then* told, 'Today salvation has come to this house' (Lk 19:9).

There are several words that are translated by 'salvation' in the Old Testament. The most common words, *yeshuah* and *yesha*, are linked with the names Joshua and Jesus and have the ideas of safety and ease, or of bringing into a 'space' where there is protection from both physical and spiritual attack. They are closely linked in thought to the idea of peace or shalom, the freedom to develop, and to create and maintain right relationships. It is certainly a 'liberating' word and not a 'confining' one. As the Psalmist put it, 'He brought me into a spacious place' (Ps 18:19).

Salvation is also closely linked in thought with the kingdom of God. It could be said that receiving salvation and entering the kingdom is virtually identical.

Salvation relates, therefore, to every aspect of life; it has a horizontal as well as a vertical dimension. But can we speak of salvation outside the church, as the statement of the Conference for World Mission and Evangelism of the WCC did at Bangkok (see page 62)?

In the Old Testament the language of salvation is applied to the whole nation of Israel and some have argued from this that salvation cannot be limited to the church or to believers. However Israel was a special nation, the people of God, and it is wiser to think in terms of the blessings of salvation being passed on to 'the new Israel', the church, at least in the first instance. To some extent it depends how a particular theologian or group is defining the word 'salvation'. It is, as we have seen, possible to use biblical words in extended ways, but it is normally wiser and makes for greater clarity if we have the same range of usage as the New Testament does. On the other hand the blessings and fruits of salvation can and should 'spill over' into society at large and God's kingdom or God's reign is wider than the church. Particularly when we speak of the end times it may well be right to apply the word 'salvation' beyond the church.[29]

The issue of how widely we can use salvation language will surface again in discussion of the gospel and other faiths in Chapter 8.

*Becoming fully human*

Another way of speaking of salvation or 'wholeness' is to talk in terms of Christ's purpose to create a 'new humanity' (Eph 2:15 NEB). The aim of the gospel is not to produce a people or a society that is totally 'other worldly' but to restore humanity to what it was intended to be; it is a programme of humanisation. The social concern track at the Lausanne II conference at

Manila in 1989 said in its report, 'The kingdom fulfils God's purpose in creation by bringing wholeness to humanity and the whole creation. In the kingdom people receive . . . a new dignity and worth . . . Those who respond to this good news . . . experience full humanity.'[30] As already noted (page 74) the papal document 'Evangelisation in the Modern World' spoke of 'transforming humanity from within and making it new'.[31]

If the aim of the gospel is to restore humanity to what it was meant to be, then our evangelism should be life-affirming and concerned with the whole of life, not just with narrow, churchly concerns. The church has sometimes seemed to justify the following lines from the poet Swinburne:

Thou hast conquered O pale Galilean;
the world has grown pale by Thy breath.[32]

What is this new humanity to be like? The fundamental model is of course given to us by the Father in the form of his Son. His disciples were often amazed at the way he treated everyone in a way that gave them dignity and worth, even women, children, the poor and others despised by society. The cross demonstrated that there should be no limits to love, and the resurrection revealed the possibility of a transformed and 'whole' existence that is both 'bodily' and 'spiritual'.

In his book *Being Human, Being Church* Canon Robert Warren uses four key words to describe the new humanity:

**Grace**, or the grace-filled life which includes material resources, beauty and wonder, the dimension of relationships and our experience of life;

**Celebration**, or the capacity to rejoice and enjoy God, life and others. It includes, but is not limited to worship;

**Creativity**, sharing in the divine nature and seeking to sustain and renew individuals, society and the cosmos. The focus shifts from an inward looking to a whole-life one;

**Community**, reflecting the love-in-community of the Trinity.[33]

## The lifestyle of the church

Lastly an integral evangelism will have implications for the lifestyle that a new Christian is encouraged to have and indeed for the lifestyle of the church as a whole. Lesslie Newbigin has argued that 'the only hermeneutic of the gospel is a congregation of men and women who believe it and live by it.'[34] The implications of the church being a sign and a pilot project of the kingdom are spelt out in Chapter 6.

The next chapter deals with the specific issues of healing and suffering.

Issues from this chapter for discussion and action will be found on page 188.

## Notes

1. George M Marsden, *Fundamentalism and American Culture* (OUP: New York, 1980), p 38. Quoted in *In Word and Deed*, the report on the Consultation on the Relationship between Evangelism and Social Responsibility, ed. Bruce Nicholls (Paternoster: Exeter, 1985), p 70.
   Originally Moody had supported social causes, but this emphasis was modified as a reaction against 'the social gospel'.
2. A phrase famously used by Karl Marx in the introduction to his *Critique of Hegel's Philosophy of Right* (1843–1844).
3. See Jesus' arguments with the Pharisees on sabbath observance (eg Mt 12:1–14, Jn 9:13–16).
4. Roger Bowen, the J C Jones Lecture, 'Rwanda – missionary reflections on a catastrophe', *Transformation*, (April 1995), p 3.
5. Quoted in Ronald Sider, *Evangelism, Salvation and Social*

*Justice* (Grove Books: Bramcote, Nottinghamshire, 1977), p 4.

6. H R Niebuhr, *The Kingdom of God in America* (Harper: New York, 1959), p 193.
7. Chris Sugden, 'Theology of Mission', *The Blackwell Encyclopedia of Modern Christian Thought*, ed. Alister McGrath (Blackwell: Oxford, 1993), p 379.
8. *Let the Earth Hear His Voice* (World Wide Publications: Minneapolis, 1975), p 5.
9. The Commission on World Mission and Evangelism, *Mission and Evangelism – An Ecumenical Affirmation* (WCC: Geneva, 1980), from the Preface.
10. *Evangelism and Social Responsibility* ('The Grand Rapids Report') (Paternoster: Exeter, 1982), p 21 ff.
11. *Living Faith in the City* (General Synod of the Church of England: London, 1990), p 12.
12. Raymond Fung, *The Isaiah Vision* (WCC Publications: Geneva, 1992), pp 28–30.
13. 'Stuttgart Statement on Evangelism' (March 1987), *Proclaiming Christ in Christ's Way* ed. Vinay Samuel & Albrecht Hauser (Regnum: Oxford, 1989).
14. Walter Wink, *Engaging the Powers* (Fortress Press: Minneapolis, 1992), pp 4–6. Not illustrated here is his first 'ancient world-view'.
15. Known as the Septuagint.
16. From a conference paper delivered at Swanwick in 1974.
17. David Bosch, *Transforming Mission* (Orbis: New York, 1991), pp 56–83.
18. William Abraham, *The Logic of Evangelism* (Hodder: London, 1989), p 107.
19. *All Are Called: Towards a Theology of the Laity* (Church Information Office Publishing: London, 1985), p 49.
20. *Evangelization in the Modern World* (Catholic Truth Society: London, 1990), paragraphs 18 and 36.

21. Jim Wallis, *The Call to Conversion* (Lion: Tring, 1983), p xii.
22. Quoted in Thomas McAlpine, *By Word, Work and Wonder: Cases in holistic mission* (MARC Publications: Monrovia, USA, 1995), p 86.
23. Quoted in Robert Warren, *Signs of Life* (Church House Publishing: London, 1996), p 3.
24. Bosch, *op cit*, p 420.
25. David Bosch, *Transforming Mission* (Orbis: New York, 1991), p 418.
26. Jim Wallis, *The Call to Conversion* (Lion: Tring, 1991), pp 6–9.
27. Roger Bowen, the J C Jones Lecture 1995 'Rwanda – missionary reflections on a catastrophe, *Transformation* Magazine (Oxford: April 1995): p 5.
28. John Wimber, *Power Evangelism* (Hodders: London, 1985), p 48.
29. There is a helpful discussion of the breadth of salvation in Chapter 4 of *In Word and Deed*, the report on the Consultation on the Relationship between Evangelism and Social Responsibility, ed. Bruce Nicholls (Paternoster: Exeter, 1985), p 85. The chapter is entitled 'How broad is Salvation in Scripture?'.
30. Chris Sugden, 'What is Good About Good News to the Poor?', *AD 2000 and Beyond* by Vinay Samuel and Chris Sugden (Regnum: Oxford, 1990), Chapter 5.
31. *Evangelization in the Modern World* (Catholic Truth Society: London, 1990), p 11.
32. Algernon Charles Swinburne, *Selected Poems*, ed. L M Findlay (Carcanet Press: Manchester, 1987), p 58.
33. Robert Warren, *Being Human, Being Church* (Marshall Pickering: London, 1995), pp 114–125.
34. Lesslie Newbigin, *The Gospel in a Pluralist Society* (SPCK: London, 1989), p 227.

# CHAPTER FOUR

# HEALING, SUFFERING AND HOPE

## *Evangelism and healing*

One of the significant developments in modern church life has been the growth of various forms of healing ministry.

This is not limited to the so-called 'charismatic' churches. Some churches arrange special healing services, while others provide an opportunity at the end of a service for worshippers to receive prayer ministry. This may be during or after a Eucharist or at another service. Sometimes it takes place at the Communion rail, but in other cases trained teams minister to people in their pews. The prayer may be for physical, mental or spiritual healing, for repentance and forgiveness, for healing of past wounds, or for wisdom and guidance in family or business matters. In some churches there is the phenomenon of 'words of knowledge' whereby team members are given messages or 'pictures' concerning particular needs among those present. The healing team may meet in the vestry prior to the service and an individual may have a conviction, for example, that someone coming to the service has a problem with their ankle. This may be announced during the service and the announcement will give confidence to the sufferer that it would be helpful to seek special prayer.

A 'picture' may be given to a team member during a time of

ministry, while their hands are touching the head of the person coming for prayer; in one instance it was a picture of a boulder which was blocking the flow of a stream. Once this was shared with the person concerned she became convicted of a problem in her life that needed removal.

The word 'healing' like the word 'salvation' can be used widely. Indeed the Greek word *sozo* in the New Testament can often be translated as healing or salvation. In his booklet *Evangelism and Healing*,[1] Stephen Skinner lists six categories:

  healing of our emotions
  physical healing
  healing of our spirits
  healing in relationships
  healing in our communities and society
  healing the whole creation.

The last three categories are discussed elsewhere, and in this section we shall be concentrating primarily on the first three. But it is important to note that the different areas where healing is needed are interrelated: a failure to forgive or to seek forgiveness may, for example, have spiritual, emotional and physical consequences.

There are a large number of questions and issues with regard to healing, but our purpose here is limited to the relationship of healing and evangelism. A healing ministry can provide opportunities for introducing those outside the church to the grace of God. In some congregations, however, the development of a healing ministry has made the church more inward-looking and Christians have become preoccupied with their own needs and with self-fulfilment. Focusing on 'me, my needs and my right to self-fulfilment' is an aspect of modern western culture, and an example of how the church can become captive to that culture. This is a criticism, rightly or wrongly, that the Rev John Wimber in 1995 levelled at the leaders of the

Airport Church in Toronto, made famous through the so-called 'Toronto blessing'.

It can be argued that until church members experience wholeness and transformation themselves, they cannot bring it to others, and that therefore an internal preoccupation when a congregation first experiences healing ministry can be justified, provided it does not become permanent. On the other hand those who have gifts of healing will develop in that ministry as they exercise it both within the congregation and outside. Bishop Graham Dow has said, 'Healing should be done in the context of evangelism: out in the streets, the work places, the homes, indeed wherever we can be with unbelievers. Too often the church has kept the gifts of the Spirit for itself.'[2] Similarly Monsignor Michael Buckley has said that 'Healing is the most powerful evangelistic weapon in the armoury of committed Christians.'[3]

There may be many occasions when churchgoers are able to invite their friends to a worship service which has a healing element to it. Very often the Holy Spirit will work in power in such a setting. On one housing estate in north London people have found healing through a number of routes – some simply through the testimony of a Christian friend, others by accepting an invitation to a Sunday service, yet others through prayer ministry in their home.

Some years ago in Paraguay the Anglican Bishop led a team that went door-to-door visiting: members of the team would knock on a door and ask those inside whether they had particular prayer needs. Very often when they made a return visit they found that prayers for healing or for other needs had been answered. This approach has also been used in other countries.

To see and experience God at work in this way is a powerful testimony to a God who is present and active in our lives – not a remote figure 'out there'. Healing is a demonstration of the gospel and is an important witness to a generation that needs to see and feel as well as hear. The former Bishop of Durham,

David Jenkins, has said, 'Our societies seem to have lost faith in any possibilities and powers either beyond human beings or deep within human beings . . . So there is a widespread collusion in an idolatry of medicine.'[4]

Certainly healing and exorcism were integral to the ministry of Jesus. The gospels are full of examples. When Jesus sent out the Twelve he 'gave them power and authority to drive out all demons and to cure diseases' (Lk 9:1). The seventy were also charged to 'heal the sick' (Lk 10:9). Similarly the ministry of the apostles described in Acts includes a strong stress on healing and miracles. Their prayer in Acts 4 is 'enable your servants to speak your word with great boldness. Stretch out your hand to heal and perform miraculous signs and wonders' (Acts 4:29–30).

Writers like John Wimber[5] argue that Jesus' healing ministry was a sign that the kingdom of God was being inaugurated. This emphasis on the kingdom, therefore, is common both to those who want to emphasise a social action dimension and to those who want to emphasise a healing dimension to evangelism. Sadly there are some who emphasise one without the other, and some of those who emphasise healing equate the church with the kingdom.

It should be noted that many healings recorded in the New Testament led to social change. After healing the lame could work, lepers would be accepted back into society and the son of the widow of Nain could support his mother (Lk 7:11–16).

Some theologians have argued that a strong emphasis on healing was appropriate in the early church as a sign of the arrival of Christ and the kingdom, but should not have such a big place today. Certainly there is much less reference to healing in the epistles and it may be that they, rather than the gospels and Acts, should provide the pattern. Healing is not explicitly included in the commissioning of the church in Matthew 28:18–20 or in John 20:21, though it could be implied. However St Paul describes his ministry as proclaiming the gospel by word and action and 'by the power of signs and miracles' (Rom 15:18–19) and there are plenty of examples of these dimensions to evangelism in the Acts of the Apostles.

There has clearly not been the same emphasis on healing in every age and in every place. This in part has been due to the church's failure to recognise the full range of gifts of the Spirit available to the believer. It may also be due to the fact that there are particular demonstrations of the power of the Spirit at different times and in different places. For example, Peter Wagner claims that 40% of the population in Brazil are practising spiritists and another 40% have some direct experience of spiritism. He argues that there is a particular need in that context for signs and wonders.[6] Similarly, Stephen Skinner argues that many in Britain today are experiencing a '*kairos* moment' in which God is powerfully at work.[7]

Certain critics of the healing movement have pointed out that in the New Testament healings were normally instantaneous, but that today healing normally takes place over a period of time and may include medical and psychological dimensions. There may have to be a period for counselling, especially when healing of the emotions is needed. However, the Spirit is sovereign and may choose to work in different ways at different times; the argument is only valid as countering a claim that modern experiences of healing are always identical with New Testament ones. It is interesting to note the claims that several have experienced an 'accelerated' experience of healing through what is often described as the 'Toronto blessing'.

As we look at the connection of healing and evangelism it is important to note that in the gospels healing is often subordinated to preaching and to the bringing of forgiveness and other aspects of salvation. In the story of the ten lepers (Lk 17:11–19) all ten are healed, but only the one who turned back to give thanks is declared to be saved. Similarly in the healing of the paralytic Jesus is concerned to emphasise the importance of seeking and receiving forgiveness. The priority of preaching is most clearly demonstrated in Luke 4 where the crowds come to Jesus for healing but are told, 'I must preach the good news of the kingdom of God to the other towns also, because that is why I was sent' (Lk 4:43).[8]

In the early days of a renewed emphasis on healing ministry some were teaching that it was God's will for all to be completely healed now, and not just in the life to come. If healing did not materialise then the sufferer was accused of lacking faith. A friend of ours who was suffering from multiple sclerosis had the last days of her earthly life made even more wretched owing to this zealous but mistaken teaching. She was made to feel that the failure to experience a cure was due to her lack of faith. Since the death of David Watson from cancer in 1984 this teaching has become less common. It is of course difficult to encourage people to raise the level of faith expectancy while at the same time acknowledging that complete healing may not be God's will for everyone all the time. The answer is to pray for wisdom and knowledge: sometimes a conviction is given that God is planning a cure and this will be instrumental in raising the level of faith.

Because of the facts of ageing and of ultimate death, complete and lasting 'health' cannot be God's purpose for us in this world. Indeed, the process of ageing may have been built into the nature of humanity, rather than being due to sin and 'the fall'. It may have been God's *original* purpose from the beginning to bring people to heaven through resurrection.[9] It is right to speak of God as healing both in this life and through death, which is the ultimate route to complete and lasting healing. Therefore if we pray for a person who is ill and they subsequently die we cannot say that God has refused to answer our prayer for healing. For the Christian, death is no longer the enemy or the end. Some years ago my sister died after a long struggle against cancer. Many from the church where she belonged prayed for her healing. Each evening two people from the congregation would sit by her hospital bed and pray with her. The prayers for healing were not answered in this life but those who visited her in her final days were amazed by an experience of the radiance of Christ at her bedside. One visitor commented, 'I had never experienced the reality of Christ in this way before.'

Although the heading of the last chapter contrasted 'pie in the sky' with 'hope on the ground', the two are closely linked. We should not be so heavenly minded that we are no earthly use, but nor should we forget that a balanced theology focuses on a hope that relates both to this world and to eternity.

There are many practical examples of churches that 'have taken healing into the community' – therapy through art and craft activities and courses in stress management are two quoted by Stephen Skinner.[10] One redundant church in London was converted into a community centre which included both a 'family area' to help deprived families under stress and a doctors' surgery. In a clinic in a secular context, a Christian doctor has to be careful not to let his or her faith become obtrusive, though there may be opportunities, when the time seems right, to use some such phrase as 'do you believe in prayer?' Those who come to a surgery within a church building, however, will not be surprised to find that prayer as well as medicine is on offer, providing a more holistic approach to their needs.

Often 'words of knowledge' can be used evangelistically. One minister tells the story of how he saw a man across the street carrying a child. He was given the knowledge that the man had deep, inner wounds. It turned out that he was a former pop star who had taken to drugs. The minister spoke to him and over the months the man came to church, experienced healing and found faith.

## The scope of the cross and resurrection

The development of an integral evangelism will affect our understanding and teaching of the cross and resurrection. These events are central to the gospel and to evangelism. The cross can be seen as an *example* or model of sacrifice and dedication. Paul uses it as a model in Philippians 2:1–11, in exhorting his readers to look to the interests of others and not just to their own.

But an aspect of the cross and resurrection that has not been emphasised so frequently in traditional evangelism is that of conquest or victory, except the victory over death. In Colossians 2:15 it is said that 'having disarmed the powers and authorities, he made a public spectacle of them, triumphing over them by the cross'. What are these powers and authorities? Some understand them as being the authorities and structures of this world; others understand them to be the demonic powers behind these structures. There seems no reason why it should not be both. Either way the clear implication is that the scope of Christ's death is not limited to the spiritual, inner realm. The evangelist should apply the teaching of the cross in terms of God's work of triumphing over sickness, defeating structural evil and overcoming injustice both through the church and directly in society. These powers are not destroyed in the sense of being removed altogether; it is rather like saying that we are between the 'D-Day' of the Normandy invasion and the 'VE Day' when the conflict was ended. Once the Normandy landing had been successfully accomplished victory was certain.

## Healing and the cross

Isaiah 53 speaks of the servant Messiah in these words: 'He took up our infirmities and carried our sorrows . . . by his wounds we are healed' (Is 53:4–5). These verses could be interpreted as referring to healing in a literal sense or they could be understood as using the metaphor of infirmity and sickness to describe sin. Some have argued that at the cross Christ overcame the power of sickness and that therefore all Christians should expect healing on all occasions. At the other extreme some have denied that it is possible to see the conquest and removal of sickness in the atonement. The third and best alternative is to argue that the presence of illness in the world is the result of sin and evil, even if individual illness may not normally be attributable to that individual's sin, and that because the cross and resurrection are God's defeat of sin and evil, all healing is part of the fruits of Christ's death. Furthermore his resurrection and our resurrection are signs that the cross is an effective victory.

## Evangelism and suffering

In the widest sense of the word, healing is central to our understanding of evangelism. But in saying this we must not imply that suffering has no place in the Christian life, or that all our problems are solved immediately we become disciples. Sometimes the problems increase or we meet new ones, though now we meet problems and pressures in partnership with Christ and find that they are used to develop our character. Modern evangelism needs a theology of suffering as well as a theology of healing and this has been one of the main themes running through this and previous chapters.

The 'Good News of Jesus Christ' is good news about a God who suffered and still suffers for our sake. Previous chapters have focused on the sufferings of Christ on the cross, but there was a dimension of suffering throughout his life and ministry. The writer to the Hebrews argues that 'in bringing many sons to glory, it was fitting that God . . . should make the Pioneer of their salvation perfect through suffering' (Heb 2:10). '. . . Although he was a son, he learned obedience from what he suffered and, once made perfect, he became the source of eternal salvation for all who obey him' (Heb 5:8–9). What does the writer mean by implying that Christ needed to be made perfect? He cannot be speaking of moral perfection because Christ is described as 'without sin' (Heb 4:15). The word (in Greek *teleioteis*) can also mean 'complete'. Christ needed to experience suffering in order to identify completely with a suffering world. This identification was symbolised by his baptism where he was especially empowered by the Holy Spirit, who descended upon him in the likeness of a dove. But Christ's experience of suffering and temptation was also necessary as part of the Spirit's equipping for ministry and mission. 'At once the Spirit sent him out into the desert' (Mk 1:9–13). His experience of suffering has also equipped him for his ministry of intercession and pastoral support in heaven: 'For we do not have a high priest who is unable to sympathise with our weaknesses' (Heb 4:15); 'Because he himself suffered when he was tempted, he is able to help those who are being tempted' (Heb 2:18). The writer is probably speaking of Christ both gaining lessons of experience and also developing his capacity for feeling. As the hymn puts it, 'Our fellow sufferer still retains a fellow feeling of our pains.'[11] Not only does Christ retain a memory of his suffering, he also suffers with us today. This must be the implication of his question to Saul on the Damascus Road, 'Why do you persecute me?' (Acts 9:4). In some sense he felt or shared the persecution of the church.

If the experience of suffering was essential in order to equip Christ for his ministry and mission then we should also expect it to be part of our experience, both to strengthen our character and also to develop our capacity for feeling. Some of the most effective evangelists and counsellors are those who have known what it is to suffer. A woman recently divorced shared her experiences with a group of women meeting in a home. She spoke of her feelings of betrayal, agony and loss of self-worth and yet of the healing that came through a fresh experience of the love of Christ. Many of those present declared afterwards that it had been the most moving evening in their experience.

The Apostle Paul stresses the importance of suffering as a tool or a school for developing Christian character '. . . we also rejoice in our sufferings, because we know that suffering produces perseverance . . . character . . . hope' (Rom 5:3–4). He develops this theme later in the same epistle. 'If we are children, then we are . . . heirs of God and co-heirs with Christ, if indeed we share in his sufferings in order that we may also share in his glory' (Rom 8:17). It is almost as if a willingness to share in Christ's sufferings is a condition of sharing in his glory.

But suffering is an experience shared not only with Christ but also with the whole of creation. The creation is described as 'groaning as in the pains of childbirth' (Rom 8:22). It seems that suffering is the pathway to transformation and to a new creation. Furthermore the Holy Spirit shares in this experience, interceding with groans of agonised longing (Rom 8:26), and so identifying with a suffering world.

It is right to speak of peace, joy and victory in the Christian life, but these promises are to be experienced as we are involved in suffering, not as we are insulated from it. It has been well said that 'some Christians grin too much (they seem to have no place in their theology for pain) and groan too little'.[12]

The example is quoted on page 60 of Archbishop Oscar Romero who was shot and killed while preaching during mass at the Roman Catholic cathedral in El Salvador. His last words, based on John 12:23–25 were. '. . . whoever, out of love for Christ, gives himself to the service of others, will live, like the grain of wheat that dies, but only seems to die'. The shock of his sacrifice and death was an inspiration to many to work for change. A hymn written in remembrance[13] includes the verse:

Take heart, fight on and never say
It's all to no avail
The rising grain's our sign of hope
That justice will prevail

Oscar Romero is a dramatic example of the transformation that can come through suffering and sacrifice.

In the third chapter of Philippians Paul describes his personal goal in these terms: 'I want to know Christ and the power of his resurrection and the fellowship of sharing in his sufferings . . .' (Phil 3:10). The order is surprising and significant; we might have expected a different order, with suffering coming before resurrection. Is there a parallel with Christ's baptism where an experience of greater power leads along a pathway of suffering before an ultimate victory?

A theology of suffering is relevant therefore not only to the content of the gospel but also to the lifestyle of the evangelist, indeed to all who seek to share the good news. If Christ had to be 'made perfect through suffering' in order to evangelise must not this be true also for his disciples today? In 2 Corinthians chapter 1 Paul describes the sufferings which he and his companions have experienced and describes this as the sufferings of Christ flowing over into their lives. But as a result they also experience the comfort of Christ and are equipped to understand, and to share in the sufferings experienced by the church at Corinth and to bring them Christ's comfort.

On one of my visits to South Africa during the period of apartheid I stayed with an Anglican bishop and his wife who had in many ways identified themselves with the sufferings and the needs of the local coloured communities. I routinely asked about the family and discovered that both his sons were in prison; they had refused to undertake national service because they knew that they would almost certainly be ordered to enter Black townships and might be given orders to fire on members of the Black community. The bishop's wife had narrowly avoided a major accident because the brakes of their car had been tampered with.

There are many less dramatic examples of Christian workers living in 'tough areas', but even those who live in more salubrious districts can find it a draining experience to enter into the feelings and sufferings of others. Archbishop Michael Ramsey called for the costly commitment of being ready to go out and put ourselves 'with loving sympathy inside the doubts of the doubting, the questions of the questioners, and the loneliness of those who have lost the way.'[14]

Evangelism is therefore inextricably linked with suffering. It is in the nature and character of our Triune God to identify with a suffering world. Suffering is an experience required of all those who seek to be partners of Christ in sharing good news.

*From sympathy to solidarity*

The call to share in the sufferings of others is firstly, as we saw on page 12, a call to sympathy in its root meaning of suffering (*pathos*) with (*sun*) others. But this does not necessarily imply an acceptance of a situation where change is possible. Christ entered our world not only to identify with it, but also to transform it. His death was not only the climax of his identification with suffering and sin but was also, with the resurrection, the initiation of a new world.

In 1995 the ecumenical London Churches Group invited two Brazilians from São Paulo to join in an assessment of a number of projects for the homeless in London. The title of their report was 'From Sympathy to Solidarity'.[15] One of the most telling comments made by the visitors was that most of the projects they visited seemed to be working *for* the homeless rather than *with* them. One of the questions asked was, 'How can we effectively welcome our homeless brothers and sisters as part of the solution rather than as the problem?'

'In Brazil we try to emphasise the active involvement of the people themselves in decision-making.'[16]

Sympathy alone can patronise rather than empower. The churches must 'find ways both of listening to the experiences of people who are or have been homeless, of defining agendas together and then of engaging in common action.'[17] The report also recommended that the homeless should be made to feel welcome in church and be given opportunities for participation in preparing worship services and in decision-making bodies.

The principles that arise from this report are of course applicable to many other situations where churches are seeking to respond to social and other needs.

*Sympathy, solidarity and integral evangelism*

We have seen how integral evangelism has a number of dimensions, including those of awakening personal faith and of sympathy and solidarity with those in social need. In the next chapter we explore how differing contexts and cultures properly shape both the content of the good news we share and the lifestyle of the church.

Material for discussion and action on issues arising from this chapter can be found on page 188.

## Notes

1. Stephen Skinner, *Evangelism and Healing*, Grove Evangelism Series No 29 (Grove Books: Bramcote, Notts, 1995) pp 5–8.
2. Graham Dow, 'Starting a Church Healing Ministry', *Healing and Wholeness*, issue no 7, July–September 1992 (Monarch Magazines: Crowborough), p 18.
3. M J Buckley, 'Our Most Powerful Evangelistic Weapon', *Healing and Wholeness*, issue no 4, October–December 1991 (Monarch Magazines: Crowborough): p 16.
4. From the Foreword by Bishop David Jenkins of James C McGilvary, *The Quest for Health and Wholeness* (German Institute for Medical Missions: Tubingen, 1981), p xi.
5. For example, John Wimber, *Power Evangelism* (Hodder: London, 1985), p 12 ff.
6. *Ibid*, p 51.
7. Skinner, *op cit*, p 4.
8. Carl Garner, *Treasure in the Field* ed. David Gillett and Michael Scott-Joynt (Fount: London, 1993), p 307.
9. John Goldingay, *Signs, Wonders and Healing* (IVP: Leicester, 1989), pp 16–17.
10. Skinner, *op cit*, pp 21–23.
11. The first line of the hymn, probably written by M Bruce (*c* 1764), is 'Where high the heavenly temple stands'.

12. John R W Stott, *The Message of Romans* (IVP: Leicester, 1994), p 242.
13. Written by the Rev Mike Walling, chair of 'Church Action for Central America' in 1996.
14. Michael Ramsey, *Image Old and New* (SPCK: London, 1983), p 14.
15. *From Sympathy to Solidarity*, London Churches Group, City Temple, Holborn Viaduct, London EC1A 2DE.
16. *Ibid*, p 13.
17. *Ibid*, p 45.

# CHAPTER FIVE

# THE LORD IS MY SHOP STEWARD

*Good News in a Variety of Forms*

*'It's not what you say, but what they hear'*

The group of men were lined up with their backs to the wall of the local bank. They wore dark suits and solemn expressions and one carried a large black Bible. They looked as if they were facing a firing squad, but were in fact 'preaching the gospel' in the local shopping centre on a Saturday morning. 'You need to be washed in the blood of the Lamb!' cried the preacher. It is difficult to know the message conveyed to busy shoppers carrying the Sunday joint, but it is unlikely that the richness of Messianic symbolism came across in the way the preacher intended!

The good news must be communicated in language that people understand. In every walk of life it is easy to slip into using jargon or technical language without realising it. The first time I dated my doctor wife she announced that she was feeling 'hypoglycaemic'. I wrongly assumed that this was a technical word for feeling romantic, but discovered that like many busy house doctors she had not had time to eat and her blood sugar level was low.

Problems of communication are not simply verbal, however. The dark suits, the stance and the expressions of the open-air witness team described above speak louder than words. They are lined up to fire verbal volleys, not to engage with the concerns or questions of passers-by – and pass by they do.

But how free are we to change the metaphors used in the Bible? We may select parables, words and phrases according to the people we are contacting, but can we employ alternatives? For example, a favourite verse with many Christians is 'The Lord is my Shepherd' (Ps 23:1) This phrase could be particularly unfortunate in Nigeria as there only the mentally ill or the educationally sub-normal are given the task of the shepherd.[1] There are probably urban areas where many would have little understanding of what a shepherd is or does. But what alternatives can we use? One suggestion has been to use the phrase 'The Lord is my shop steward.' This has a contemporary ring, but not everyone will feel that it is the best illustration of caring leadership. More fundamentally the word 'Lord' will seem strange to many today: in Britain it may be associated in people's minds with a judge in a law court or with a member of the House of Lords and if so will not convey quite what is intended.

Even the opening words of the Lord's Prayer – 'Our Father' – can have negative associations for some. They may have suffered from an uncaring or even brutal father. Some will want to be more radical and begin the Lord's Prayer with the words 'Our parent' or 'God our Father and Mother'. The safer approach, however, is to treat the word as a 'given', but to give it more positive associations. After all there must have been some uncaring fathers in New Testament times. But the masculine words used of God need balancing with some feminine ones. There are biblical examples such as Matthew 23:37 where Jesus compares himself to a hen wanting to gather *her* chicks.

Issues of language and image have been familiar to missionaries working in other parts of the world for many years. The Roman Catholic missionary Vincent Donovan discovered that the Masai tribesmen in East Africa had no word in their language for God. He believed that the nearest 'dynamic equivalent' was their word for lion.[2] In another part of the world missionaries translated 'faith' with the word used by a tribesman for sitting down in a chair and trusting his weight to it.

The task is to communicate the treasures of the gospel in the language and thought forms of the recipient. But this is a matter not only of straight 'translation', but also of themes and content.

## Good news in a variety of forms

A number of evangelistic training schemes and booklets have advocated a simple summary of the gospel. An old favourite has been the 'ABC' of the gospel where 'A' refers to admission of sin and guilt, and 'B' to belief and trust in the death of Christ for our forgiveness. 'C' is for the commitment of discipleship. There are arguments for producing a simplified summary that can be memorised, but the dangerous assumption behind such summaries is that every individual can and should be approached in the same way and has similar needs.

Jesus did not use a standard package. So much so that in the book *Youth Culture and the Gospel* Pete Ward entitles one of the chapters 'Why doesn't Jesus preach the gospel?'[3] By 'the gospel' in this title he means a traditionally truncated summary of the 'ABC' variety.

The gospel has to be shared in a wide variety of contexts and cultures and so must take different shapes and forms. This was so in Jesus' teaching ministry. He certainly challenged people to repent, but his approach to those who were poor or needy was one of welcome and acceptance. In our fragmented modern society where many feel devalued or worthless, the first piece of good news to share is that each person is of value to God. To begin by describing them as 'wretched sinners' is to crush them still further. In many cases the initial focus of the conversation with Jesus was a need for physical healing.

A range of approaches is used, for example in John Chapter 1. Jesus is variously introduced as the Lamb of God, the one who baptises in the Spirit, the Messiah, the Son of God and the

King of Israel. Even so the range of language in this chapter is limited because all concerned are Jews who are familiar with Old Testament language and symbolism.

There is variety, too, in the Acts of the Apostles. The way the good news is expressed to Jewish groups is very different from the way it is expressed to Gentiles. The addresses given by Peter to the crowd at Pentecost (Acts 2), by Stephen to the Sanhedrin (Acts 7) and by Paul to those in the synagogue at Pisidian Antioch (Acts 13) can be contrasted with Paul's addresses at Lystra (Acts 14) and Athens (Acts 17). The first three are addressed to Jewish audiences and are rich with Old Testament references and ideas; the last two use the general themes of creation, providence and history. At Pisidian Antioch Paul says, 'We tell you the good news: What God promised our fathers he has fulfilled for us, their children by raising up Jesus. As it is written in the second Psalm . . .' (Acts 13:32–41). At Lystra the crowd believe that Paul and Barnabas are gods and want to offer sacrifices to them. Paul insists that they are only men and urges his hearers to turn to the living God who created the earth and gives rain and crops (Acts 14:11–17).

As the gospel spread to the Gentile world there was a diminishing emphasis on Jesus being the Christ or Messiah and a greater one on Jesus as 'Lord', a rival to other lords, and ultimately to Caesar himself.[4] At the same time there is a decreasing mention of the 'kingdom of God'; such a phrase could be politically dangerous. It is not so much that the basic gospel is being altered, but that it is being clothed in a different language and different facets are emphasised according to the need of the hearer. A helpful analogy is that of a lock and key. The evangelist needs to determine what shape key will unlock people's minds to the grace of God.

## What is culture?

The task of translating the gospel into different languages and ideas is part of the cluster of issues that come under the heading

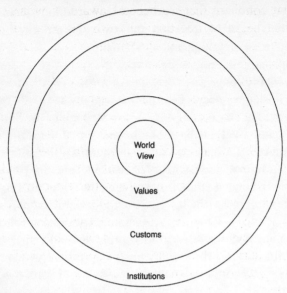

*Figure 11*

of 'gospel and culture'. But what is culture? It can be described as 'the compound of customs, priorities, values, assumptions and beliefs shared by a social group or community'.[5] Or it can be shown as a number of concentric circles:

The inner core is a society's or group's world-view – it might be capitalism, Marxism, materialism or something else. Then come values, such as the importance of family life, or of the worth of the individual. Next come customs, some of which may be value-free, such as driving on the left. In the outer circle come institutions such as Parliament, and the church.

Often a person has to stand outside a culture in order to understand it; we find it difficult to assess the culture in which we are immersed. There is a Chinese proverb that says, 'If you want a definition of water don't ask a fish.'[6] This is why exposure to others' cultures helps us to distinguish what is particular from what is universal; it is when we visit Africa, or receive a visitor from that continent that we become aware of cultural differences and begin to question our own customs, values and beliefs. What we have assumed to be universally true may only be appropriate for certain contexts.

A distinction can also be drawn between different levels of culture, which we might term general, specific and personal. An example of a general or global culture is western secularisation. Because of superior economic and technological power, western secular culture has in practice dominated many other cultures. The Big Mac and the can of Coke are virtually universal. Examples of specific cultures within a country would be rural, urban, youth, black, etc. But people often live in a mosaic of overlapping cultures. An urban black teenager who works in a bank, likes reggae music and watches television will probably have a personal culture which is a mix of urban, black, youth, banking, reggae, television etc.

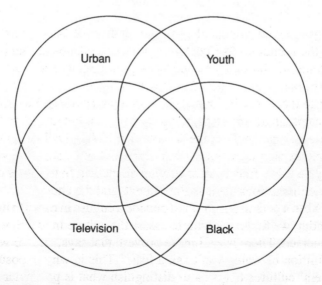

*Figure 12*

*Gospel and culture – a range of relationships*

Because we can more easily understand culture 'from outside', gospel and culture discussions often begin from two-thirds world contexts. The early missionaries differed in their reaction to the variety of customs and cultures they encountered, though with the benefit of hindsight we can see that they rejected too many of the local customs and exported too many of their own. Some of the exports were fairly obvious, such as the institution of archdeacons exported by Anglicans and the provision of harmoniums by all and sundry. Less obviously, missionaries brought certain assumptions about authority and styles of leadership and about ownership of land and resources that were foreign. Not that the decisions were always easy. Harmoniums were substituted for drums in many parts of Africa, but then drums had an association with witch doctors. There are parallels in the West. It was some while before guitars were used in traditional churches, partly because of their association with what some felt to be undesirable music.

One of the factors in the rise and growth of the African Independent Churches was the feeling that too much of African culture had been rejected. In Asia the local cultures were not rejected to the same degree. Bishop Michael Nazir-Ali has argued that this may have been because much Asian culture had similarities with European culture, having books, organised religion and a hierarchically ordered society.[7]

Historically there have been four main relationships between the gospel and cultures:

rejection
assimilation
incarnation
transformation.

*Rejection*

Clearly there will be some aspects of cultures which must be rejected as contrary to the gospel. An extreme example was the custom in India of burning a widow alive on her husband's funeral pyre. It can be argued that some other customs may not be ideal in the light of the Gospel but need not immediately be rejected; an example would be the custom found in parts of Africa of men and women sitting separately. Indeed this was the custom in some English university Christian Unions in the 1950s.

Bishop David Gitari of Kenya argued at the 1988 worldwide Lambeth Conference of Anglican Bishops that in Africa polygamy is a custom that need not be rejected straightaway. Not all would agree. The problems posed by polygamy, however, are as much practical as theoretical. What is to be done if a man who has more than one wife comes forward for baptism? In principle he should keep the wife he first married and put away the others. But how soon should this be done and what support can and should be given to those wives who are put away? In such societies, a woman on her own, neither a daughter in her parents' home nor a wife living with her husband, can suffer great hardship.

There are also examples where some forms of traditional Christian culture have been unnecessarily rejected. In the West new worship groups may deliberately or thoughtlessly mask traditional Christian symbols with large overhead projector screens and drum kits when they could easily allow both to be prominent.

*Assimilation*

It has been argued that in some sections of the church in the United States the gospel has been assimilated to the American way of life. One commentator notes 'the evangelical Protestant subculture has been overrun by the general American culture's values. If divorce rates have risen in the general culture, they have also risen among evangelical Protestants . . . [They] follow a similar pattern of TV viewing, of materialism, and other cultural changes.'[8]

Similar comments could be made about Britain, Australia and other Western countries.

We have seen in Chapter 4 how healing is a ministry that can be an effective accompaniment to evangelism, but an excessive concentration on healing can be a form of assimilation. We live in an individualistic culture which is obsessed with personal health, development and enjoyment. Two church courses were advertised under the titles 'I want happiness now' and 'Feeling good about feeling bad.' One form of such assimilation is the so-called 'prosperity gospel' where those who become disciples are promised that their commitment will automatically lead to greater health and wealth.

## Incarnation

It is difficult to see how a 'prosperity gospel' can be squared with the lifestyle and teaching of one born in a stable and dying on a cross. As the Word made flesh Jesus identified with the human race and gave new worth and value to it. The very incarnation demonstrates how God is determined to identify with our suffering world. Jesus models or demonstrates what the 'new humanity' is to be like. He identified not just with the human race in general but with the specific Jewish culture of first-century Palestine. In doing so he showed how the good news has to be translated or incarnated into specific cultures. Similarly Paul declared that he was prepared to be 'all things to all men' (1 Cor 9:19–23) for the sake of the gospel. He was willing to live like a Jew in order to win Jews and like a Gentile in order to win Gentiles.

A word that is frequently used in this connection is 'contextualisation' – relating the good news to specific contexts and cultures. In practice its range of meanings largely overlaps with that of 'incarnation'.

## Transformation

Although Jesus was incarnated into and identified with the culture of his day he was also prepared to be critical of it. His positive attitude to women, to the poor and to those looked down on by the religious establishment, for example, was contrary to many of the attitudes of the time.

Ideally both the message and the messengers of the gospel will reject what is wrong about a culture, identify with what is good and ultimately transform it for the better.

### Gospel and culture in Europe

Gospel and culture questions are not limited to the two-thirds world or to the Middle East. The same issues arose when Christianity came to Europe. There were those like the Benedictine monk Boniface who was sent to evangelise the Germans and tended to destroy the old to make way for the new. He destroyed pagan temples, and in Hessen in 724 he had an old oak, dedicated to the pagan god Donar, cut down in the presence of a crowd of spectators. On the other hand Pope Gregory soon came to the contrary view that anything not in conflict with the gospel should be preserved. He sends Augustine to evangelise the English and tells him (c 601 AD) to destroy idols, but not the temples in which they are worshipped. If the temples are well-built then they can be purified from devil-worship and dedicated to the service of the true God. This line had its negative as well as its positive results. Christianity in some parts of Europe became just a religious veneer over pagan animism. Hence the title of Anton Wessels' book on the subject, *Europe: Was it Ever Really Christian?*[9]

No evangelism or theology can be totally culture-free. Many European theologians have assumed that western theology is objective and culture-free and have looked down on Third World theologies as being syncretic because they relate theology to context and culture. Anton Wessels argues that European theology is also affected if not conditioned by European culture.[10] Nor can church life be totally culture-free. It could be argued that there is a proper 'universal' church culture in the sense that new converts are rightly expected to adapt to such strange activities as worship, the Eucharist and Bible study. But the exact form of worship will vary from culture to culture. We need to distinguish the universal from the particular, and often we can only do that as we encounter worship in a variety of cultures.

## The gospel and western culture

Although there is a wide variety of cultures in the West we are all affected by the general or global culture of Western secularisation. Bishop Lesslie Newbigin has argued[11] that secularisation is a child of the eighteenth-century period known as 'the Enlightenment', when there were significant developments in science, art and thought. As science and technology developed, the intellectual and practical need for God diminished. It was assumed that science would eventually meet every need and answer every problem. The issue was not so much whether God existed or not – if he did exist he had no relevance in a modern scientific society.

Enlightenment culture, according to Bishop Newbigin, makes a basic division between 'the public world of scientific facts' which must be accepted as undisputed reality, and 'the private world of religious opinions'. These opinions are a matter of individual choice and are subjective and relative.

The German theologian Wolfhart Pannenberg has argued that the causes of secularisation are due not so much to the Enlightenment but more to the disenchantment with Christianity that arose as a result of the religious wars of the sixteenth and seventeenth centuries.[12] This disenchantment has continued into the twentieth century bolstered by conflicts in Northern Ireland and Bosnia which are perceived as religious in origin.

Whatever the main causes of secularisation are, however, the distinction between scientific facts and religious opinions clearly holds sway today. This distinction is not one, moreover, that influences only the intellectual elite as it penetrates to every part of society. On television, for example, scientific 'fact' is presented by an 'expert', perhaps dressed in a white coat, whereas religious opinions are the subject of a debate or discussion, with the studio audience being left with the feeling that they cannot be sure about any of the views expressed. 'Religion is more often than not bracketed with those issues which are in some way contentious and disruptive . . . [it] is very often seen as a cause of social conflict and a cloak for deep-seated racial or social prejudices.'[13]

One of the urgent tasks for evangelism, therefore, is not only the evangelising of individuals but also of 'modern' Western culture. The task is both to affirm what is good and to expose its weaknesses and inconsistencies. The latter task has been made easier by the fact that the balloon of technological triumphalism has already been pricked by an increasing awareness of the damage done to the ozone layer, to tropical rain forests, and to human health in our polluted cities, as we saw in Chapter 1. It is no longer assumed that science has all the answers.

One of the fruits of the Enlightenment has been an increasing specialisation, individualism and fragmentation, making it almost impossible to have a coordinated 'overview'. This has increased the difficulties faced by those concerned to tackle the needs of deprived inner city areas, for example.

In many branches of science it is being recognised that theories have to begin with a number of hypotheses which rest ultimately on a stand of 'faith', and that absolute objectivity is impossible. It is difficult to examine objects and situations without in some way affecting them – to take an everyday example, the fish will not behave normally if I put a hand in their bowl! No scientist is absolutely free from assumptions and prejudice.[14] It is therefore argued that the distinction between religious 'opinion' and scientific 'fact' is overstated and that science does not so much 'prove' as 'probe'.

## Postmodernism

The questioning of Enlightenment 'certainties' and increasing doubts about some of the earlier claims of science and technology have been factors in the emergence of a new culture which is not easily describable, but which has been given the title of postmodernism. The recognition that the powers of reason are limited, for example, has led to a growing emphasis on experience.

There are good aspects in this trend, it is important that any study programme links teaching with experience. In the past some ministers have given lectures on prayer, without giving the 'audience' the opportunity to experience the different styles of prayer. On the other hand an over-emphasis on experience can be at the expense of rationality.

There is similarly a growing interest in spirituality, which in itself is good, but this is sometimes at the expense of doctrine.

Many are turning from a mechanistic view of the universe to a search for the transcendent, though the search has often ended up with astrology or with the 'new age' movement. Another contributing factor in this search has been the disillusionment with the false hopes held out by both communism or capitalism, and by the recognition that economics is not an exact science. In 1984 *The Economist* magazine asked three groups of people to draw up economic forecasts for the year 1994. One of the groups was four London refuse collectors whose forecast proved to be more accurate than that of the group of finance ministers and the group of chairmen of multi-nationals.[15]

Some observers call the culture in which we are now living 'post-modern'. This is characterised by a multi-levelled and fragmented society. Within this society the exiling of moral and religious beliefs into the 'private world of opinions' has led both to pluralism – a belief that there are a number of possible choices – and relativism, a belief that there is no absolute truth, but that everything is only relatively true, if true at all. The question is not, 'Is it true?' or, 'Is it right?' but, 'Is it true for me?' or, 'Does it feel right for me?' There is a choice from a bewildering variety of teachings and moralities which has been illustrated by a supermarket analogy. Just as the shopper is faced with a choice of breakfast cereals, so people can go shopping for religious and moral values in the 'supermarket of ideas'. Some shoppers have a 'pick 'n mix' approach, selecting a range of ideas from different faiths and belief systems. In this way some will select a number of Christian teachings and mix with them a belief in reincarnation. Many who do this will fail to realise that reincarnation is not part of Christian teaching. The singer Peter Gabriel had his two children 'christened' into six different religions at the Self Realisation Fellowship in Los Angeles.[16]

Very often ideas or symbols are detached from the original settings which gave them meaning; they are reduced to images and then given a new and different meaning. The pop star Madonna, for example, uses religious language and wears crucifixes.

How does the evangelist approach the modern secularised person? As with any relationship between gospel and culture there will be some aspects of postmodernism that should be rejected, some that can be accepted and some that can be transformed.

Although the Christian cannot accept the notion that there is no ultimate reality we have argued in this chapter that our understanding of that reality can be affected by cultural factors.

The emphases in evangelism needed in modern Western society can be summarised as follows:

Affirmation and not just challenge
Dialogue and not just proclamation
Process not just crisis
Local not just national
Personal not just broadcast
'Whole life' and not just 'spiritual'
Experience not just words
Group not just individual

## Affirmation, not just challenge

This emphasis was described on page 106. To those who were deprived, insecure and powerless Jesus' first words were positive and affirming, conveying a sense of worth and value. A classic example is that of the woman of Samaria who encountered Jesus at a well (Jn 4:1–7). Although Jews despised Samaritans and refused to use the same drinking vessels, Jesus' first words to her were, 'Will you give me a drink?'

## Dialogue and not just proclamation

Modern approaches to evangelism are focusing less on a 'microphone' evangelist as an authority figure: there is still a need for proclamation, but the main emphasis is on dialogue and a concern to listen, learn and understand before speaking. As we shall see in Chapter 8 dialogue is appropriate as we encounter those of other faiths. It is also important in our relationships with those who do not profess any faith. Those involved in evangelism need to learn from the approaches in education that are learner-centred.

## Process not just crisis

General ignorance of the Christian faith and the fact that on average people take four years to come to faith, necessitates an approach that is one of 'process, not just crisis'. There will often need to be crisis points and challenges in a person's faith journey, but one of the best metaphors is that of 'journey' – a journey that in some senses the Christian evangelist and his or her friend are on together. Not 'come and listen to me' but 'let us explore the faith together'. This is sometimes described as 'an Emmaus style of evangelism'. The account in Luke's Gospel describes how Jesus walked to Emmaus with two disciples, encouraged them to share their hopes and fears, and waited for an invitation to enter their home before revealing himself

(Lk 24:13–32). The 'journey' approach seeks to avoid any implication that Christians have already 'arrived' and have nothing more to learn.

## Local not just national

The postmodern reaction against authority has been accompanied by a distaste of centralisation. This is why one of the emphases of the Decade of Evangelism in England has been on the local and on diversity. Even the nationwide programme 'On Fire', celebrating Pentecost 1994, provided resources and a national logo, but encouraged churches in each locality to develop their own activities. A plurality of approaches, styles of worship and church structures is essential. This will mean openness to other traditions, rather than the defensiveness that focuses on simply preserving our own.

## Personal not just broadcast

While mass communication can be extremely valuable in preparing the way it has been shown time and time again that personal contact is vital for a person to come fully to faith. The 1994 'Minus to Plus' campaign to distribute an evangelistic booklet to every household in Britain probably owes its relative lack of success to this factor more than any other. Had there been a longer time of preparation, greater effectiveness in developing a partnership with the churches, and a programme of personal visits to follow up the distribution the story might have been very different.

## 'Whole life' and not just 'spiritual'

Postmodernism tends to replace the fragmentation of modernism by seeking a 'holistic' approach. We are now putting things together again, having taken them apart, and trying to see life whole. Having destroyed parts of the environment by unbridled capitalism (and communism) we are now respecting nature and even, in the case of some new-agers, worshipping it. The need for a holistic approach in mission and evangelism has been argued in Chapter 3.

## Experience not just words

A secularised society is a society free from church control, not necessarily one where religion and spirituality are absent. Although only a small proportion of the population attend a Christian church, a high proportion have some belief in God and pray. They may often turn to a spiritual pot-pourri under a New Age umbrella. To those who are disenchanted with materialism and are searching for a dimension of transcendence, the church needs to offer a spirituality which is real and relevant, not simply a doctrinal formula.[17]

A high percentage of populations in the West do not habitually read. Yet many of the churches use approaches that are intellectualised and stuffed with words. As a graffiti comment at the end of a church conference put it, 'The Word became words . . . and choked'. There have to be words – the good news has been communicated to us through the Scriptures, but even within the Bible there was a great variety in the approach used. On the one hand we have Paul's epistles which even the Apostle Peter described as difficult in parts – on the other we have the pictorial form of parables used by Jesus and often presented through drama today.

But the good news is pre-eminently communicated through a person, the living Word. Even the Apostle Paul did not limit his communication to words. As noted on pages 92–93 he spoke of having shared the gospel 'by what I have said and done – by the power of signs and miracles, through the power of the Spirit' (Rom 15:18–19). We might sum it up with the phrase, 'sharing the good news through witness, words, works and wonders'. The reason why many charismatic churches are significantly growing today may in part be due to the fact that charismatic life and worship relates well to a postmodern culture. The same can be true of a congregation which demonstrates the love of Christ through community action.

## Group not just individual

In some cultures it is important to evangelise communities or groups rather than individuals. This has been the approach in several overseas countries in the past. In parts of Africa, for example, the premature baptism of an individual could have resulted in him or her being cut off from their family and tribe. Sometimes missionaries waited until a whole tribe was ready to come to faith. There are also examples in British history: the Celtic missionaries would seek to evangelise whole tribes and at the end of the sixth century AD the tribe of the Cantuare in Kent was baptised as a result of the evangelistic work of St Augustine. But there are also contemporary examples where traditions of solidarity make a group approach vital. Some teenagers find their identity in the relationship they have with their peer group – for an individual to become a Christian on his or her own will cut them off from their friends. It may be better to work with groups of friends rather than with individuals and to wait until the group as a whole or a majority of it are ready for Christian commitment.

Some adult cultures also have this solidarity. The Anglican churches in the Liverpool area have produced a leadership course that is designed for training leaders as a group rather than as individuals. Local church councils are invited to put forward a small group for training rather than an isolated individual.

## Culture and the evangelist

The principle of incarnation means that the evangelist and all who seek to witness to the good news must aim to enter the worlds of others – their thought forms, ideas, hopes and fears. This may mean relocation – to an overseas country, for example, or to a deprived area in their own country. It may simply mean taking up a new hobby or interest. This is St Paul's approach of becoming 'all things to all men'. An example of this principle was Paul's willingness to go through purification rites in the Temple (Acts 21:17–26). However he was adamant that forms of identification with particular groups should not in any way prejudice the gospel.

There are of course practical questions as to how far identification is possible and desirable. Not all missionaries to China in Hudson Taylor's day followed his example of wearing Chinese dress. Pete Ward argues that while it is important for older Christians to get alongside teenagers today by taking an interest in their concerns and by being ready to listen to their music, it is not essential and they will lack authenticity if they pretend to be trendy or to like their music.[18] Authenticity is often more important than 'cultural correctness'.

On one occasion I travelled back from a conference with a Ghanaian minister on a London Underground train. Almost immediately he struck up a conversation with the passengers sitting near him and took the opportunity to share his faith. It is not normally part of British culture to talk to strangers on public transport and certainly not on the London Underground during the rush hour. Yet because he showed a genuine interest in others his initiative came across as authentic and not intrusive, but allowance was no doubt made because he was patently from a different culture. It was another demonstration of the value of cross-cultural friendship and partnership.

## *Culture and the setting for evangelism*

As we have seen from Chapter 4 we must be prepared to go onto others' territory and not simply invite them onto ours, to be pre-pared to go to others' homes or to visit community centres, clubs and pubs. When he went to a town Paul often started by preaching or initiating dialogue in the synagogue, this was his deliberate policy of 'to the Jew first'. He was concerned that his own people should hear the good news and in a sense his own people had been prepared through the law and the prophets to have the foundation knowledge for hearing and understanding the gospel. But often they rejected the message and Paul went on to the market place (Acts 17:17), the house next door (Acts 18:7) or to a lecture hall (Acts 19:9). We need to find parallel places today. A church in the centre of England regularly hires a room in a pub for supper and discussion. A housewife paid regular visits to the local swimming pool and was able to build friendships with a group of women she encountered there.

Some enquirers' courses are designed to be taken into people's homes. However in some areas it is not part of the culture to invite others into a home and it then becomes necessary either to overcome the cultural barriers or to use a local club. A group of churches in south east England regularly study the lonely hearts column of the local newspaper and ring round in order to invite people to meet up in a nearby public house.

One youth worker found himself relating to a group of young people in the centre of England. They met in a bar, rather than on church premises, but were able to use a room out of hours where they could create their own worship, writing poems, composing songs and leading discussions on the Bible.

*Culture and lifestyle*

There are cultural issues in the approaches used for nurture or discipleship training. It is sometimes said that churches expect new Christians to take on middle-class culture in order to be part of local church life.

Many churches expect people to be familiar with committees, paper, and keeping diaries. Some years ago a black South African complained that his church synod was dominated by the whites because it used a 'Western' committee approach that loaded the meeting in their favour. The same might be said in other countries where there is a mix of social groupings but where meetings tend to get dominated by middle-class members.

Dave Cave, speaking from the experience of leading a

congregation in a deprived area in Liverpool, argues that the middle-class person tends to speak rationally and logically, 'whereas the working-class person has more of a tendency to speak from emotional impulse.'[19]

Different cultures have varying approaches to time-keeping. It has been said that 'Europeans have watches, but Africans have time.' An African is likely to arrive late for a meeting if he encounters someone on the way who needs an unhurried chat. The European would have looked at his watch and broken off the conversation at a vital point. The African may start a worship service late, but will not be in a hurry to finish it. As one African put it, 'You Europeans will start worship on time whether the Holy Spirit has arrived or not.' Europeans suffer from what has been described as 'the enslavement of punctuality'.

There are also cultural differences in the matter of morality. In both the preaching of the gospel and in the nurture of those who respond there can be a disproportionate emphasis on what is sometimes described as 'middle class morality'. This morality will tend to have an emphasis on personal honesty, whether, for example, we arrive at work on time, take home the office pencils or use the phone for personal calls. There may be an inadequate stress on matters of justice, whether, for example, the firm is almost exclusively concerned with making profits and has little or no concern for people.

It is not always easy to determine whether particular forms of traditional Christian behaviour are being dictated by culture or by the gospel. In the case of teenagers, for example, the best way forward will be to initiate an open debate or discussion.

## Culture, teaching and the Bible

We need to be aware of two cultures or two groupings of cultures when we read the Bible. First there are the cultures of the original writers. Second there are the different contemporary cultures of those who read the Bible today. There are frequent debates on whether particular instructions given by St Paul were intended to be universal commands for every person in every age or commands for a particular culture. St Paul gave instructions, for example, that women should keep their heads covered in church (1 Cor 11:3–10). Few people would feel that this command is binding today, though there have been generations of men and women who have.

When we read the Bible today we tend to wear the spectacles of our contemporary contexts and cultures. When first-world Christians read Isaiah Chapter 6 they usually focus on the possible reference to the Trinity in the phrase 'Holy, Holy, Holy' (Is 6:3) whereas many two-thirds world Christians will focus on Isaiah's ministry to challenge oppression. Similarly with the story of Elijah in the cave (1 Kings 19): first-world Christians will think of the hymn 'Dear Lord and Father of mankind . . . speak through the earthquake, wind and fire, Thy still small voice of calm.' Many two-thirds world Christians will focus on Elijah's revolutionary task of changing governments by anointing new kings over Syria and Israel (1 Kings 19:15–16).

John Drane tells the story of visiting a group of Christians who lived on a huge garbage tip in Manila in the Philippines. They undertook a Bible study on the story of the Good Samaritan and the leader asked all those present to identify with one of the characters in the story. First-world Christians would be likely to choose the priest, the Levite, the innkeeper or the Good Samaritan himself, but the person most of the Filipinos chose was the man attacked by robbers. They saw themselves as victims while most first-world Christians would identify with one of the authority figures.[20]

An awareness of the different cultural spectacles that can be and are worn as we read the Bible is vital for evangelists who want to share the good news in a culturally appropriate way.

## Limits to flexibility?

Some Christians are understandably nervous at this point. If the writers then and Bible readers today are all affected by the different cultures in which they live how can we trust the 'Bible message'? Are we making the task of Bible reading so difficult that we can only come to the Bible through scholars?

The first point to make is that we can get a clearer grasp of the Bible's teaching by comparing one part with another – it is always dangerous to try to interpret a passage of the Bible out of context of the whole. The second is that the same Holy Spirit who inspired the original writers guides us together with Christians through the ages and across the world. We should be slow to reject an interpretation that has been accepted by Christians through history. Today we become aware of our cultural blinkers when we compare how those of other centuries and those of other contemporary cultures interpret Scripture. This is why interchange between those of different cultures is so important.

Finally there is a clarity in the Scriptures that enables the poorest of the poor sometimes to have a clearer picture than those blinded by wealth or education.[21] Raymond Fung speaks of the 'ability of the poor to handle and understand the Bible directly without a hierarchy of teachers and experts.[22]

Bishop John Saxbee's fascinating book *Liberal Evangelism* is sub-titled 'a flexible response to the Decade'. He rightly argues that evangelists should learn to listen and not just proclaim[23] and that listening to people in different contexts and cultures will or should transform the presentation, if not the content, of the gospel. On the other hand he admits, with refreshing honesty, that many liberal Christians have been so busy 'transforming' the gospel that they have forgotten to transmit it.

John Saxbee admits that there is a danger of substituting our own ideas or of rewriting the gospel: he quotes a story[24] told by Dennis Nineham about the Baptist scholar T R Glover. Two Oxford dons were talking together:

'Have you read Glover's autobiography?'

'I didn't know he'd written one.'

'Oh yes, he has. It's him to the life. Only for some reason he's called it *Jesus of Nazareth*.'

On the other hand it can be too simplistic to talk in terms of 'an unchanging gospel in a changing world'. Canon Robert Warren has argued that some of those who emphasise 'the unchanging gospel . . . have been least aware of how their understanding is shaped by their own culture.'[25]

Whenever we enter into dialogue with others, whether people of another faith, common religion, or of no faith, there is always the possibility that we shall begin to see new facets of the gospel. This theme will be developed further in Chapter 8.

It may be that it is our understanding of the gospel that is changing rather than the gospel itself, but we need to check with Scripture, the tradition of the church and with Christians of differing cultures that our understanding is authentic. The Church of England report *Good News in Our Times*, sub-titled 'the gospel and contemporary cultures', recognised this danger and drew up 'Ten signs of Authenticity'[26] as a test of whether a transformation of the gospel in understanding or presentation is authentic.

## Entering others' worlds

If we are to 'proclaim afresh' the faith 'in each generation'[27] we need to enter others' worlds, after the pattern of Christ who was determined to identify with our suffering world. This will have a radical effect on our understanding of how the gospel relates to contemporary society and on our lifestyle. It may mean personal sacrifice or suffering, or at least a willingness to enter into the sufferings of others. It should also, as we shall see in the next two chapters, have a radical effect on the lifestyle and programme of the church.

Material for discussion and action on issues arising from this chapter can be found on page 189.

## Notes

1. Pete Ward, *Youth Culture and the Gospel* (Marshall Pickering: London, 1992), p 36.
2. Vincent Donovan, *Christianity Rediscovered* (SCM: London, 1978), p 63.
3. *Ibid*.
4. This is elaborated by Michael Green, *Evangelism in the Early Church* (Highland: Crowborough, 1990), Chapter 5.
5. *Good News in Our Times* (Church House Publishing: London, 1991), p 41.
6. Lesslie Newbigin, *Foolishness to the Greeks* (SPCK: London, 1986), p 21.
7. Michael Nazir-Ali, 'Culture, Conversation and Conversion', *AD 2000 and Beyond: a Mission Agenda* ed. Vinay Samuel and Chris Sugden (Regnum: Oxford, 1991), Chapter 3, p 27.
8. 'Keeping in Step: How Far will American Evangelicals Follow Secular Cultural Trends?', *Pastoral Renewal* (October 1984): p 34, quoted by John Wimber, *Power Evangelism* (Hodder: London, 1985), p 48.
9. Anton Wessels, *Europe: Was it Ever Really Christian?* (SCM: London, 1994).
10. *Ibid*, p 15.
11. See for example Lesslie Newbigin, *The Gospel in a Pluralist Society* (SPCK: London, 1989).
12. Wolfhart Pannenberg, *Christianity in a Secularised World* (SCM: London, 1989), pp 3–19.
13. Jim Mcdonnell, 'Mass Media, British culture and Gospel Values', *The Gospel and Contemporary Culture*, ed. Hugh Montefiore (Mowbray: London, 1992), p 159 ff.
14. This has been well demonstrated by Bishop Lesslie Newbigin in his book *The Gospel in a Pluralist Society*, *op cit*, and especially in Chapter 3.
15. Quoted in *The Times*, May 1995.

16. Graham Cray, *From Here to Where?: The Culture of the Nineties* (Church of England Board of Mission: London, 1992) p 14.
17. *Ibid*, pp 16–19 suggests the themes of community, journey, spirituality and pluralism as appropriate for a post-modern age.
18. Ward, *op cit*, p 48 f.
19. Dave Cave, *Jesus is Your Best Mate* (Marshalls: Basingstoke, 1985), p 119.
20. John Drane, *Evangelism for a New Age* (Marshall Pickering: London, 1994), p 37 ff.
21. This is the Reformation teaching on the 'perspicuity' of scripture.
22. Raymond Fung, formerly the Evangelism Secretary of the World Council of Churches, writing in his Newsletter of April/May 1990.
23. John Saxbee, *Liberal Evangelism* (SPCK: London, 1994), p 13.
24. *Ibid*, p 23.
25. Robert Warren, *Being Human, Being Church* (Marshall Pickering: London, 1995), p 103.
26. *Good News in Our Times*, *op cit*, p 36.
27. A phrase that comes in the Church of England service for the Consecration of Bishops, *The Alternative Service Book* (Hodder: London, 1980), p 387.

CHAPTER SIX

# GOD'S PILOT PROJECT

*The Church as a Sign of the New Humanity*

### The forbidding church

The young couple were proud of their newborn baby and went to church to thank God for him. The birth had been something of a miracle. As the doctors battled to save both mother and child the father stood outside the ward and in desperation began silently to pray. He was not a church-goer and would not have called himself a Christian, but during that prayer he had a vision of Christ. So it was natural to come to church, but far from easy. As they entered the dark medieval building the congregation, mainly elderly, looked round in surprise. Later, as the baby started gurgling, the surprise turned to disapproval. But the couple persevered. They realised that Sunday attendance would not be enough. Over the new few months the wife helped with a sale of work and the husband joined a men's working party to do odd jobs round the church. But apart from polite greetings no one came alongside, and no one offered hospitality. They never felt welcomed and moved away.

For some churches the problem is not so much how to attract people, but how to avoid putting off those who do make an approach. How, in fact, to be attractive rather than forbidding. We frequently meet people who claim to have rejected the gospel because they have had a negative experience of a congregation or of a church-goer. It may be a colleague at work, a friend, a neighbour or a relative, someone who has claimed to be a Christian, but who has been thoughtless, dishonest or unloving.

It is little use trying to share good news if we are bad news. Gandhi is reported to have said, 'I would be a Christian if I could see one.' Research has shown that there are many today, especially young people, who have little time for the church but are attracted by the figure of Jesus Christ.

In defence it can be said that we are invited to put our faith in Jesus Christ rather than in the church, and that by definition the church is a company of sinners. Jesus himself said, 'I have come to call sinners, not the righteous to repentance.' He used the analogy that only those who recognise that they are ill will come for healing. In one sense it is no more surprising to find imperfection in the church than illness in a hospital. Yet it is unfortunate if those called to advertise good news of lives changed by the gospel show little sign of it. It is like a salesman who advertises washing powder while wearing a dirty shirt. We don't expect people in hospital to be the picture of health, but if there are few signs of improvement and recovery hard questions are bound to be asked about the credibility of the treatment.

*The church and the gospel*

In this chapter we explore the relationship of the church, those called to be 'good news people', to the gospel and to evangelism. There is a sense in which the church is, or should be, part of the good news. Yet in the past some theologians have argued that Jesus Christ came to announce a new kingdom rather than to found a church and that we should be working for peace and justice in the world rather than recruiting new members. The argument draws on the first words of Jesus recorded in the Gospel of Mark, 'The kingdom of God is near. Repent and believe the good news!' (Mk 1:15).

It is true, as we have seen from Chapter 3, that some of those who have emphasised church growth as central to evangelism have omitted or underplayed the kingdom dimensions of the gospel. But it is clear that when Jesus called people to follow him they did not follow as isolated individuals, but were formed into a gospel community. This community, the church, was designed to be a sign or foretaste of the kingdom – the new society or new humanity where God's rule over every aspect of life is acknowledged or displayed.

The church should not be equated with the kingdom. God's work and reign can be discerned in the world at large, but it should have a lifestyle that demonstrates kingdom values such as love, justice and peace. It can therefore be described as a pilot project to demonstrate what an ideal society should be like, or as a laboratory where ideals can be worked out in practice. Too often the practice is, of course, far from the ideal. At an adult membership class the candidates were asked what influenced them to consider joining the class. One volunteered the answer, 'I was so impressed on coming to this church that people were not like Christians.' The remark was meant as a compliment but it implied that their experience of Christians hitherto was of a people who were joyless and unfriendly.

## The church as a sign of the new humanity

Ideally the church should be the place where the gospel is lived or seriously attempted. Where this happens it can be a living demonstration of the new humanity. The letter to the Ephesians sets out God's master plan for the world as 'bringing all things in heaven and on earth together under one head, even Christ' (Eph 1:10). Within that plan God's people are described as a 'single new humanity' (Eph 2:15 NEB), citizens of a new country and members of God's household (Eph 2:19). The phrase 'new humanity' or 'one new man' (NIV) is significant. The church is designed to be the start of a new humanity – not the narrow, other-worldly, or peculiar organisation that is often on display, but an attractive fulfilment of God's original intentions for the human race. This is why effective evangelism has to start with the renewal of the church. The life of the early church is described in Acts 2:42–47 as centring on fellowship, teaching, the Eucharist, prayer and praise. They met in homes and also in the temple. They experienced wonders and miraculous signs. They shared the whole of life together, including their possessions.

The passage ends by saying, 'The Lord added to their number daily.' The sharing of possessions did not continue, at least not to that degree, but the principle that a renewed church attracts new members continues to be valid.

A teacher in the centre of England found faith when she started helping in a summer playscheme at the local church. 'Instead of finding sombre faces, dressed in "Sunday bests" I met ordinary yet warm, friendly and happy people who made me feel very welcome. The love and warmth that the group showed drew me on to wonder if they had actually got something that I was missing out on. Could they be right and I was wrong about their faith in God?'

Eventually she came to faith herself.[1]

## Disciples and not just converts

In contrast to those theologians who want to substitute the kingdom for the church are those evangelists who emphasise the individual's conversion experience but underplay the importance of the church, even though they acknowledge the need for 'follow-up' and 'nurture'. This is a particular danger for specialist evangelistic organisations: they can be tempted to become 'para' or substitute churches. When they fall into this trap it is partly the fault of those traditional churches that fail to demonstrate a zeal for evangelism.

In recent decades the word 'evangelism' was often associated with major campaigns, mass meetings and 'crusades'. For practical, if not for theological, reasons the evangelist saw his task as limited to the work of bringing people to faith. The 'follow-up', nurture and discipleship was the responsibility of others. Evangelism has been seen primarily, if not solely, in terms of 'proclamation' rather than in terms of discipling.

However the church growth movement which began in the United States and which has been associated with the names of Donald McGavran and Peter Wagner re-emphasised the terms of the Great Commission in Matthew 28:16–20, 'Go and make disciples of all nations, baptising them in the name of the Father and of the Son and of the Holy Spirit, and teaching them to obey everything I have commanded you.' It was argued that evangelism must include not only proclamation of the gospel and winning converts, but also the task of incorporating them into the church. We have seen in Chapter 3 (page 72) that even this interpretation of the Great Commission and its application to evangelism needs supplementing, but the argument is valid so far as it goes. John Wesley argued that it is impossible to have 'solitary Christians' and established class meetings to provide the necessary nurture. In 1748 he and his helpers refused to preach unless a society was in existence or could be established to care for those who responded.[2]

Evangelism should therefore include both proclamation and incorporation. This implies a strong teaching element.

*Evangelism as both proclamation and teaching*

In the 1930s C H Dodd sought to show that the early church made a definite distinction between preaching (*kerugma*) and teaching (*didache*).[3] He drew out from the speeches in the Acts the core of the *kerugma* as focusing on the birth, life, death, resurrection and return of Christ. The distinction is helpful, but not as watertight as Dodd suggested. The Apostle Paul spent considerable time debating and teaching in certain cities and it would be difficult to draw a clear line between his preaching and teaching.

The apostles and many of the disciples featured in the gospels grew in faith as a result of significant periods of teaching. While it is true that many Jews made an immediate response of faith in the early chapters of Acts, they were then incorporated into a regular programme of teaching. Furthermore, most would already have had a deep understanding of the Old Testament promises which Christ came to fulfil. This was not so with the Gentiles then, and it is not so with the majority of the population in the West today.

There is a need for a strong teaching element in evangelism in the West today, for practical as well as theological reasons. It cannot be assumed that people have the same basic knowledge of the Christian faith that earlier generations had. A survey conducted in England in 1955 showed that 83% of adults over sixteen claimed to have attended Sunday School or Bible Class for several years in their childhood. A further 11% had attended for a short time and only 6% had never attended. Probably two-thirds of the nation's children were in Sunday Schools in the 1930s and the 1940s. But the 1989 English Church Census revealed that on a typical Sunday only 14% of children under fifteen were in a church-related activity of any denomination.[4]

This can be paralleled elsewhere. Sunday School attendance in New Zealand in the primary age band has fallen from 169,000 in 1960 to 19,600 in 1992.

Ignorance of the Christian faith is illustrated by the story of the customer in a shop looking at a display of crosses and crucifixes. When the assistant asked which one she would like she replied, 'I rather like that one with a little man on.'

The need for evangelism to include teaching and nurture is emphasised by an important piece of research into how people come to faith. Bishop John Finney has shown that people take on average four years to come to faith and that the biggest factor is not so much missions and special events but friendship.[5] These conclusions have significant implications for evangelism strategy. Until comparatively recently it was assumed in some sections of the church that the strategy for evangelism was to bring in an evangelist and have a mission. In many congregations, however, it was discovered that more people came to faith through the regular programmes of the church.

For these reasons, teaching programmes that give enquirers an opportunity to come to faith over a period are to be welcomed. Examples include the Roman Catholic rite of Christian Initiation, 'Alpha', 'Good News Down the Street' and 'As we go'.[6]

## The place of missions

This is not to say that there is no longer a place for missions and other events. Missions can be extremely effective when a local church involves large numbers of its members and refuses to leave all the responsibility to an incoming team. The test of any mission is whether it leads to ongoing evangelism, or whether local church members flop back exhausted at the end. Research into two particular missions showed that church attendance was lower some months after the missions than before they started. Missions should be like a peak on a climbing graph line of evangelism, not a climax or culmination. In recent years local events in halls and homes have tended to be better supported than large central meetings. Where these local events can be repeatable and reproducible there is greater impetus and modelling for an ongoing programme of evangelism. Examples of reproducible events include evangelistic supper parties and men's breakfasts. A special supper party or breakfast held during a mission can be the first in a series.

The late David Watson said that evangelism should be automatic, spontaneous, continuous and contagious.[7] He argued that there are remarkably few exhortations to evangelise in the epistles and that this was because evangelism was assumed to be part of the normal daily life of the early church.

The relevance, style and effectiveness of missions is closely related to the context in which churches are set. The 'crusade' or large meeting approach depends to some extent on there being a significant 'fringe' of people who have links with their local church but are not yet committed disciples. In recent years a director of a North American evangelistic organisation commented that crusades were becoming less effective even in the United States because of a shrinking fringe.

*A centre of hospitality*

Congregations that want to evangelise need to become and to create centres of hospitality.

As noted in Chapter 2 (page 42) the idea of hospitality is central to the Christian faith. Jesus frequently accepted invitations to meals, even from those who were his critics, and used them as opportunities for discussion, teaching and evangelism.

When Levi or Matthew the tax collector became a disciple, he laid on a meal in order to introduce his friends to Jesus (Lk 5:27–29). This is a model for evangelism today. New converts often have a web or network of relatives who have not yet considered the Christian faith. With the help of maturer Christians they may be able to provide a supper where they can sensitively testify to their new-found faith. Many of the new enquirers' courses such as 'Alpha'[8] include a welcome meal or meals as part of the programme.

Hospitality was one of the themes of the 'On Fire' project in England at Pentecost 1994. Local groups of churches were encouraged to mount a party to celebrate the birthday of the church and to invite people along from the community around. At Pentecost 1995 the churches in London organised a project called 'The Great Banquet'. A banquet held in central London was the catalyst for a number of smaller 'satellite' banquets held in a hostel for the homeless, a derelict church, a local park and other places. There was an emphasis on inviting the homeless and others in need, but also on providing an opportunity for representatives of the churches and of the local communities to talk together about the needs of the area.

## Welcome and acceptance

Whether a meal is included or not the principle of welcome and acceptance is central to many forms of evangelism. We saw on page 41 how this is a dimension of the good news we share.

Welcome and hospitality are particularly important in an age of depersonalisation. A congregation that has a welcome team, with people who are gifted at remembering names, can give newcomers the sense of being valued and important. Welcome and acceptance are also demonstrated when newcomers are given the opportunity of exercising ministry. One of the secrets of the phenomenal growth in Pentecostal churches throughout the world has been the emphasis on 'every member ministry'. Our era is one where the average person feels of little worth or value. To be given an opportunity of ministry and service is an important demonstration that God values each individual.

This hospitality and acceptance has implications for the over-coming of class, social, racial and religious divisions. These were significant issues in the early church. The Apostle Paul worked hard to break down divisions not only between Jew and Gentile (see page 42) but also between the rich and poor. He criticised the rich who brought large packed meals to church while poorer members of the congregation went hungry (1 Cor 11:17–22). In Rome there were some Christians who were extremely scrupulous over what food they ate and which special days they observed. Others were far 'freer' or more 'flexible'. Paul challenged both groups to be open to one another and to be ready to adapt their practices for the sake of each other with the words 'Accept one another, then, just as Christ accepted you' (Rom 15:7). Accepting and giving hospitality to those of different backgrounds, views and practices is a vital witness to the good news that Christ has accepted them and us.

This acceptance is a demonstration of the new humanity where divisions of race, class and gender are overcome and all are one in Christ (Gal 3:28). Desmond Tutu, the Archbishop of Cape Town, speaks of 'the rainbow people of God', where the different colours blend together to make a beautiful whole.[9] One of the many ways in which this was demonstrated in the old South Africa was the involvement of Christian medical and educational workers, whites and blacks together, in black squatter camps such as 'Crossroads'.[10]

A more earthy picture than the rainbow is that of the stew. It is a useful analogy as it illustrates that harmony and unity do not mean uniformity. The church is to be a stew, where the different components retain their identity but share their flavours with one another. It is not like a soup where the component parts lose their identity.

## Welcome and acceptance, yet challenge

There are occasions, however, when it is far from easy to balance welcome and acceptance with the need to present the challenges of the gospel. Jesus tended to vary his approach according to the needs of the person. He comforted the disturbed, but was also prepared to disturb the comfortable. He was ready to challenge religious leaders and the wealthy, like the rich young ruler (Lk 18:18) who wanted to belong, but ended up belonging to his belongings. But he was especially gentle with the poor and the marginalised. In this he was fulfilling Isaiah's prophecy that the Messianic servant would not break bruised reeds or snuff out smouldering wicks (Is 42:3) – he would gently fan into flame a weak faith. This is one reason why Archbishop Robert Runcie described the Church of England as follows: 'Ours is not a church with hard edges; it is the church of the smoking flax.'[11]

## Worship and evangelism

Worship and mission are the two primary activities of the church, but how do they relate? Worship can and does motivate worshippers to evangelise, but how far are worship services events that can be used for evangelism? The traditional parish mission was a series of mid-week services geared for particular groups such as those married in church over the previous five years. Today this approach has limited success. Special occasions such as Mothering Sunday, Harvest and Christmas carols are still a draw in many areas for those who do not attend church regularly. One rather tactless minister ended a Harvest service held at the end of September by wishing such people a happy Christmas.

The Family Service movements have been attempts to draw whole families to church on a more regular basis. There has been significant success, though a recent report suggests that these movements may have integrated the children of church-going parents at the expense of children whose parents do not attend.[12] The latter now feel alienated, especially when as a result of the Family Service policy the Sunday School has been abolished. A strong theological case was made for bringing the whole family together in church, but as always theological theory has to be tested by practice.

Recently a number of experimental services for young people have developed in several parts of England. One example is called 'Holy Disorder'[13] which has a disco atmosphere with smoke and laser lights, but a greater reverence and depth than many adult services. While some experimental services are noisy, a number include periods of silence and parts of Greek Orthodox and other liturgies.

In many districts a new housing estate has been built which is some distance both geographically and culturally from the main church of the area. In some cases a new congregation or 'church plant' has emerged,[14] meeting in a school, a bar or a community building on the estate. A new 'church plant' starts without a tradition and is therefore freer to experiment with new forms of worship, ministry and leadership. In Chester-le-Street, in the north of England, the parish church planted a number of such congregations in housing estates. The worship there was notable for relating to local community needs and those leading had local accents rather than middle-class imported ones.[15]

An interesting approach to evangelism has been developed in the United States under the title 'Seeker Services'. These originate from the Willow Creek church in Chicago. Because the general population think of Sunday as the day for worship, even if they do not usually come themselves, the Willow Creek leaders decided to move the regular worship and teaching for their committed members to midweek but to provide an occasion on Sunday mornings when members could bring their friends. The 'Seeker Service' is a presentation of the Christian faith which includes drama, interviews, teaching and songs, but not the full range of normal worship.

There is a real question as to how far these events can be described as worship or 'services'. Significantly the church building is described as an 'auditorium' which implies that those present are there to hear and to spectate rather than to participate. There have been adaptations of the Willow Creek approach in England, some using 'neutral' premises such as hotels. It is not clear how much of the success of 'Willow Creek', which is set in a middle-class Chicago suburb, depends on a North American culture where church-going is more normative than in the West as a whole, and where people are prepared to listen without participation. About 42% of the population of the USA is churchgoing, compared to 10% in Britain.

It should be noted that experimental youth worship and Seeker Services can demand a good deal of commitment in terms of time – for prayer, planning, preparation and team building – and that not every congregation will have the resources to achieve the standards that the average person expects.

The 'Seeker Service' approach raises the fundamental question – What forms of worship, if any, are appropriate for the non-Christian? The church at Corinth seems to have had 'outsiders' coming in to their worship services. Paul warns the church (1 Cor 14) to make sure that the worship is intelligible to such people, but he assumes that the newcomer will be struck by a sense of God's presence and will exclaim, 'God is really among you!' When Paul describes the Eucharist as a proclamation of the Lord's death (1 Cor 11:26) he may well have had in mind an evangelistic dimension. If we isolate gospel presentations and teaching from worship we are in danger of assuming that most people respond to the gospel in a purely cerebral way.

John Drane, in arguing for a strong link between evangelism and worship, has said, 'Much modern psychology has reached the . . . conclusion . . . that a sense of mystery, discovered and expressed through something like worship, is basic to the human condition.'[16]

## Prayer, worship and the Spirit

Luke constantly links together prayer and worship with the gifts and outpouring of the Spirit for mission and evangelism, both in the third gospel and in Acts. The disciples are described as being 'constantly in prayer' in the days leading up to Pentecost (Acts 1:14). Later Peter and John are imprisoned. Once released they hurry to re-join the other disciples. Far from advising caution they worship together and pray for renewed boldness. As the Spirit is poured out, the place where they were meeting was shaken (Acts 4:31).

Worship and prayer are also the context in which guidance is given in selection of missionaries and in choice of priorities for mission. It was after the church met for worship and fasting that Barnabas and Paul were chosen for special work (Acts 13) and later Paul was given a vision to cross over into Macedonia (Acts 16:6–10).

Those congregations which are effective in evangelism today are usually those that give priority to forms of worship and prayer that have reality and relevance, and motivate for mission.

*The church as a sign and a part of the gospel*

We saw in the last chapter how the good news needs to be presented in a variety of forms and in this chapter how the church, the people of God, is central to the work of evangelism.

In the next chapter we explore how the church and its programmes need to take a variety of forms.

Material for discussion and action on issues arising from this chapter can be found on page 189.

## Notes

1. Philip King, *Making Christ Known* (Church House Publishing: London, 1992), p 6.
2. William Abraham, *The Logic of Evangelism* (Hodder: London, 1989), p 54.
3. See, for example, C H Dodd, *The Apostolic Preaching and its Developments* (Harper and Row: London, 1936).
4. *All God's Children?* (Church House Publishing: London, 1991), p 3 ff.
5. John Finney, *Finding Faith Today* (Bible Society: Swindon, 1992).
6. *As We Go* has been produced by the Chichester diocese of the Church of England.
7. David Watson quoting R Halverson in *I Believe in Evangelism* (Hodder: London, 1976), p 134.
8. The Alpha Course is produced by Holy Trinity Church, Brompton, London.
9. Desmond Tutu, *The Rainbow People of God* (Bantam: London, 1994).
10. Crossroads was a squatter camp in Cape Town that was eventually bulldozed by the authorities.
11. Archbishop Runcie in a speech to the General Synod of the Church of England; November 1990.
12. *All God's Children, op cit*, p 8 ff.

13. 'Holy Disorder' is a youth service, started by a group in the Gloucester diocese of the Church of England, and used in churches within the diocese and beyond.
14. 'Church Plants' are described more fully in the next chapter.
15. Described in *Good News in Our Times* (Church House Publishing: London, 1991), p 88.
16. John Drane, *Evangelism for a New Age* (Marshall Pickering: London, 1994), p 119.

# CHAPTER SEVEN

# BODY SHAPES

*The Church as a Variety of Forms*

The people who lived in the housing estate sometimes looked across the busy dual carriageway to the parish church on the other side, but to them it seemed a different world. It was inaccessible both literally and culturally. The congregation at the parish church were middle-class and used to reading; they collected a pile of books and leaflets every time they entered on a Sunday. But they were concerned for people on the estate and recognised that it was little good expecting them to make the cultural leap in order to join them for worship. The church council therefore invited a world mission agency to set up a small group of volunteers who would live on the estate. Slowly contacts were made and a small children's club started. This grew and moved to the estate community centre where eventually all-age worship began.

Chapter 5 illustrated how the good news has to be shared in a variety of ways; this chapter illustrates how the church, the gospel community, has to be prepared to be reshaped in a variety of forms in order to share that good news.

## Light and salt – gathered and dispersed

The Sermon on the Mount uses two vivid images of the church – that of light and salt (Mt 5:13–16). The light image suggests that the members of the church should be *gathered* together in a loving community where the quality of their life – meek, merciful, pure and peacemaking (Mt 5:3–10) – shines like light in darkness. The salt image suggests, however, that church members should also be *dispersed* into society. There they are to bring the qualities of salt – purification, protection from corruption and 'flavour' into every part of life. Just as salt has to penetrate food in order to be effective, so the church and its members need to penetrate society. Jesus also used the picture of yeast being mixed into a large amount of flour so that it worked through all the dough (Mt 13:33). This image suggests a steady, but hidden transformation of society from within.

Too often we have implied, if not taught, that active Christianity is almost entirely centred within church premises. We have emphasised the 'gathered' but not the 'dispersed' mode. In many congregations the week's activities advertised in the 'notices' are almost entirely those taking place on church premises. Sermon illustrations of dedicated Christian living focus on these activities and on prayer and Bible reading, but not often on daily work or community life. This is one of the dangers of a paid professional ministry that does not have to enter the world of work. Howard Snyder has argued that while the Reformation transformed the concepts of the mass and of priesthood, it did not adequately tackle the concept of the temple or of the church building as the centre of ministry and witness.[1] Temple-centred Christianity is well illustrated by the nineteenth-century mission compound. The compound fence preserved an oasis of Western culture. Outside the fence were the natives' huts. Inside were the mission clinic, school and church and the houses of the missionaries. There was, of course, a need to take certain precautions for reasons of health and safety, but the degree of distancing was unnecessary. In at least one part of Africa the natives were not allowed inside the missionaries' house but had to hold conversations on the verandah.

It is easy to be critical with hindsight and from the comfort of a critic's armchair. We also need to confess that the compound mentality is present in much twentieth-century Christianity in the West. Where a church building is established activities naturally centre on it. That is why a missionary priest refused to build a chapel when he first arrived in a Central American village. He began by advertising the fact that he was willing to celebrate mass, on request, from house to house.

'Compound Christianity' can be illustrated by the story of the minister who persuaded a new Christian to give up his training evening at the rugger club in order to join a study group in the church vestry. As a result his friendship links with the rugger club were severed and a significant opportunity for evangelism lost. Where the model of discipleship is a 'compound' one the result can be a dull, flavourless Christianity.

Too often we have had a concept of lay ministry which almost entirely centres on compound or temple activities. We have harnessed captains of industry to give out hymn books. When the Bishop arrived to take a confirmation service in one church the minister introduced a middle-aged member of the congregation as 'the senior server'. He failed to mention that he was also the chief executive of the Local Health Authority. Both activities could be described as ministry, but compound Christianity will focus on the few hours spent on ministry in the compound to the exclusion of the week spent on ministry in the world.

Howard Snyder has also argued that while the Reformation radically altered the concepts of priesthood and the mass it did not fully alter the style of leadership – authority simply moved from altar to pulpit. The perpetuation of old-fashioned authoritarian leadership can hinder the recognition of the importance of lay leadership, whether in the compound, in the home or in the world. It is still possible to find a minister rejecting a layman's offer to run a Bible Study in his home with the words 'I don't believe in laity leading Bible Study without a minister present.' With these concepts of temple and leadership it is difficult for many laity to capture the vision and gain the confidence to penetrate society and to share the good news.

## Bridges into the church

In using the word 'church' it is often assumed that what is meant is the gothic building on the corner of the street and that 'bringing people into church' means bringing them to a Sunday service. In practice it is often more effective to introduce friends to 'church' in the form of a 'bridge group', designed to welcome those who are not ready to come to worship. Examples include enquirers' groups meeting in a house, and 'parent and toddler' groups or 'drop-in centres' in church halls.

Sometimes there needs to be a greater clarity as to the aims and purposes of such groups. Some have a value in their own right as meeting social needs in the community. Some are intended as bridges into the parent congregation. Others may be designed as bridges to hearing and responding to the good news, leading perhaps to the founding of a new-style congregation as quoted at the beginning of this chapter. It is often helpful to hold a 'mission audit' in order to determine what is happening. In one case such an audit revealed that the church members in a parent and toddler group were so busy dealing with play equipment and coffee that they had no time to get alongside parents coming in from outside the church. Yet their aim had in part been evangelistic. A bridge group is misnamed if there is no one crossing the bridge.

There are also a number of bridge or para-church organisations which operate nationally, sometimes focusing on students[2] or youth. The relationship between such organisations and the churches is varied and complex, but one important test of a student organisation, for example, is how successful it is in preparing students for joining in 'normal' as opposed to student church life after leaving college.

*Beyond the fringe*

If the research project 'Finding Faith Today'[3] is right in saying that most people come to faith through friendship then it is even more vital that church members are encouraged and released to build friendships in the community. We have already seen how the lifestyle of many congregations is 'compound centred' (pages 146–147). For some this provides a safer and less demanding option: by crowding our lives with 'compound' activities we have an excuse, or think we have an excuse, for avoiding the challenge to join Christ in his mission to the local community. As Jack Burton has put it, 'The best place to hide from God is in the local church.'[4]

In the past, congregations have often had a significant 'fringe' of those who have children in the Sunday School or youth organisations or who attend Sunday worship two or three times a year at major events such as Harvest, Christmas and Mothering Sunday. Most traditional forms of evangelism and missions 'fish the fringe' but do not reach beyond it. But in many areas, the fringe is shrinking fast and in some it has disappeared altogether. Congregations therefore need to have 'go' strategies as well as 'come' strategies, to be centrifugal as well as centripetal. So much of what we call 'outreach' is in fact 'indrag'. The task is not primarily to say 'come onto our territory, to hear us tell you our message' but to go to their territory, to engage with their issues, from a Christian perspective. The church needs to have an 'incarnational' approach to evangelism, with its members being willing to enter others' worlds just as Christ entered our world. These worlds include those of work and industry, of sport and leisure, of the local community and of the media. The task will include not only witnessing to personal faith but also seeking to relate the gospel to issues of the day.

But how can the church provide a support structure for its

members in these worlds? Membership of a house group can give opportunity for sharing problems and encouragements, for prayer and for general ministry. In some congregations the leaders have invited those in particular spheres, such as education or medicine, to meet with them and to share work experience and theological insight; on occasion this has led into a Sunday presentation and discussion for the whole congregation. One minister in London asks members of his congregation if he can join them for a day at their workplace. This is not feasible in every case, but where it is it gives the minister an appreciation of the issues being faced. The church member feels that his or her work is being taken seriously and will have a significant opportunity to discuss the problems and opportunities that he or she faces.

In some areas churches have set up groups for Christian parents and teachers. Where there is a major local industry it may be possible to arrange discussions with church members and others who are workers or managers. It is less easy in a large conurbation where church members travel a distance and undertake a variety of jobs. Where it is not possible for a congregation or group of local churches to set up an appropriate specialist group it may be necessary to have one at regional or national level. Some professions have national networks: examples in England are the Christian Medical Fellowship and 'Christians in Sport'.

*Church in a variety of shapes*

The Church of England is one example where church life has been organised on a territorial basis. The minister or vicar is given the 'cure (or care) of souls' of all those living in a designated area called 'the parish', though it is recognised that some will already be affiliated to other churches. There are examples of other denominations who have worked on a geographical basis, though not with such a tight parish structure. In a mainly rural society, where the church on the village green is seen as the centre of the community, geographical structures are appropriate. But they are less satisfactory in urban areas where people have a choice of church and where members of different congregations drive past each other on the way to worship. It is even less satisfactory in large conurbations where the workplace may be some distance from the home and where the circles of work, family, leisure and church may hardly overlap. The early church did not have our modern separations between church, home, work and community. Some church members would be part of the household of a Roman villa which was both the workplace and the home.

But people today live in a mosaic of different worlds and cultures. Different forms of church life have been developed to take account of these changes. There may be congregations, cells and networks of particular cultures, interests and responsibilities. There are the networks for medicine and sport quoted above. Other examples include networks of Christians in industry and government. Within a locality there may need to be a specialist congregation for young people or for a particular ethnic group. For young people in particular, the traditional style of music and the practice of sitting in rows and listening to an authority figure leading from the front, can be alienating. The issues are even more acute where there is a difference of race and language as well as of culture. One church in London arranges worship in Tamil and Urdu, and another in Wolverhampton has an Asian service in Punjabi on Sunday afternoons. This is particularly important for older women who may have been virtually housebound and whose English is very limited. Once a month the Wolverhampton church has a united service in both English and Punjabi in order to bring the different language groups together.

Local territory cannot any longer be seen as the only basis for church life, and the parish system is being radically modified. But in some areas the local is still extremely important, especially with an increase in unemployment and in the practice of working from home. In some cases the home has become what has been described as an 'electronic cottage' with a member of the household having a modem link with computers at his or her firm.

Yet at the same time the need for creative thinking and flexibility is now greater than ever before. An extreme example of flexibility and mobility is the church 'youth bus' bought and equipped for youth work in a large area of a city in the centre of England. Few of the churches in the area have the resources to initiate and maintain youth work, but by working cooperatively they have provided an opportunity for effective work among young people. The bus is parked in different locations each night of the week and visited by young people in that area. The vehicle has one area for relaxation and discussion, and one for a disco.

### 'Missionary congregations'

The church needs to be structured for mission and evangelism, not just for pastoral care. In 1967 the World Council of Churches published a revolutionary document on church structures under the title *The Church for Others: the Missionary Structure of the Congregation*. It was argued that 'in a pluralistic world the structures of the church must be pluriform since the church tends to take its shape in relation to God's activity in a pluriform world.'[5] 'Ministering fellowships or little congregations will thus be fashioned in very diverse shape to enable Christians to be present in all spheres of life, in order that they may participate in mission, not as an occasional activity but as their very *raison d'etre*.'[6] A number of examples of cells and networks in industry and in other parts of life, not too dissimilar from those quoted above, were explored in the report.

There are two current programmes on missionary congregations within the British Isles. One is a Church of England programme, and the other an ecumenical one set up by the Council of Churches for Britain and Ireland. Both are designed to research into the factors which enable congregations to become missionary. It is clear already that a relevant spirituality and effective leadership are key factors.

In some cities the mission policy has been to develop a city centre mega-church, drawing in members of the congregation from all over the city. There are certain advantages of size in that this kind of church is able to provide a variety of evangelistic and training programmes. But the danger is that members of these large congregations can become passive spectators who are not involved in their local communities. Spreydon Baptist church in New Zealand decided on a very different strategy. The church is based in a working-class suburb in Christchurch, and as the congregation grew in numbers it looked for a site for a larger building. They were unsuccessful. 'Out of heart-searching and prayer came the conviction that we should solve our space problem by starting neighbourhood congregations . . . the congregations have kept us in touch with the grass roots of community life. And the total church gives us the resources for effective mission.'[7] The church now has a range of social projects.

*Third World base communities*

In Brazil, and in many other parts of the world, new forms of church life have sprung up, especially in the Roman Catholic church. The traditional pyramid structure with power and authority flowing down through Pope, Bishop and Priest to the laity (see Figure 13) is being questioned. There is a chronic shortage of priests, and so clusters of laity have been formed in *favela* or shanty town areas: they meet for worship, study and action. Bible Studies tend to have applications that relate to social as well as to personal and religious dimensions. The communities are lay led and so the focus is on water shortage as well as worship, on drains as well as doctrine. The priest, who has to serve a large area, visits to administer the mass, but also to provide support.

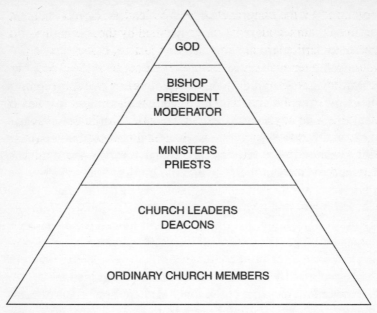

*Figure 13*

There have been attempts to form base communities in the
North. Not all have been successful. The secular North, especially in Europe, is a very different context from Brazil where
most of the population has a natural 'God awareness' and where
there is a much larger 'fringe'. Some experiments have lacked
a spirituality at the centre. Another factor may be that there is a
greater visible contrast in Latin America between the poverty of
the shanty towns and the wealth of the rich; as a result people
are more motivated to work for social change. However there
are some good models in the North such as the one quoted at the
beginning of this chapter.

Basic Christian Communities (BCCs) must be distinguished
from house groups or special interest groups. House groups are
not the *basic* unit of the church – the congregation is. The house
group meetings are extra to a range of activities and meetings

organised by the congregation and its leaders. Special interest groups within a congregation are formed by those who want to promote particular concerns such as justice, care in the community, prayer and renewal. But very often the same people are involved: 'the different groups overlap each other, forming a common core of activists, while the great majority of people do not belong to anything'[8] (see Figure 14).[9] The basic Christian community, however, is the fundamental unit of the church. It is the primary, basic meeting or activity, rather than an extra for those so inclined.

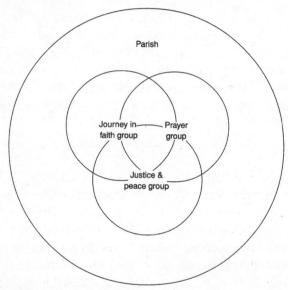

*Figure 14*

Another helpful illustration is a cosmic one (see figure 15).[10] The sun is the parish and its busy agenda, with regular church members circling round it like planets. The comets are members of the fringe who appear once or twice a year or even once or twice in a lifetime for baptisms, weddings and funerals. The outer space represents those who have no connection at all.

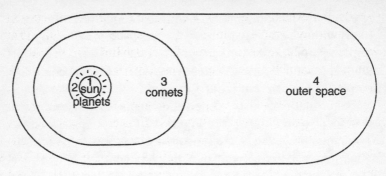

*Figure 15*

Figure 16[11] however represents a situation where a large number of basic communities have been created. In area 4 they form 'missionary bases' for such matters as race relations, environmental concerns and care in the community. These missionary bases may include both those who are church members and those who are not.

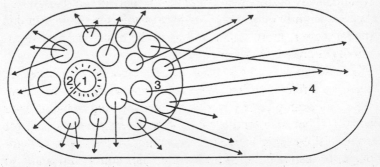

*Figure 16*

An example of such a missionary base can be found in John Reader's *Local Theology*.[12] John formed a 'Local History Society' that looked at the past history and present situation in a part of rural England in order to relate history, theology and local life with a view to promoting action for change. John

Reader believes that the church can have a valuable ministry in a community simply by providing a 'space' where different concerns can be aired and shared. It can also link together different networks in a community, effectively becoming 'a network of networks'.

One form of basic Christian community life is that of the cell group church. 'Truth and Liberation Concern' is a Christian community in Melbourne, Australia, which has formed a cell-group structure that seeks to be culturally accessible to those around, particularly to the poor and to the younger 'street people'. Their ministries include crisis, marriage and family counselling, emergency accommodation and a single-parent support group.[13]

The idea of the cell-group church has been popularised by Ralph Neighbour who divides his time between being a part-time Baptist pastor in Singapore and a lecturer in the United States.[14] In his model the cell group is again the basic unit of the church, not an optional extra for the keen. These groups are led by unpaid lay pastors who are linked or 'networked' by salaried pastors. Rightly or wrongly the impression is given that in this model there is more 'control' than in the basic Christian community approach from catholic roots.

It is not so easy to find basic Christian communities that are workplace related rather than local community related. There are many examples of Christian groups meeting in factories or hospitals, but they tend to polarise between groups set up for prayer, Bible study and evangelism and groups set up to campaign for justice issues. Third world basic communities aim to include both agendas. One work-related cell group can be found in a hospital in the north-east of England. It meets for fellowship, prayer and study, but also looks at issues affecting the daily life of those working in the hospital. It has been able to bridge the different groupings within the hospital – management, doctors, nurses and support staff – and is often consulted by management as having a more comprehensive and more objective overview than many of the other hospital groups can possibly have.

## Homogenous or multicultural?

In the early days of church-growth theory it was argued strongly that a homogenous congregation, a congregation of the same social and racial group, was far more effective in evangelism than a 'mixed one'. A white, middle-class congregation would be able to appeal to people of a similar background outside the church. It is unhelpful, so the argument went, for enquirers to have to make a cultural leap in joining a congregation as well as meeting the challenges that are integral to the gospel. There is strength in this argument and it is normal practice in local churches to have organisations which have a particular appeal for specific groups such as men, women, teenagers and young children. It can also be argued that there are already different cultural forms of worship on a Sunday in a large number of churches. In some there is the 8 o'clock traditional and reflective service for those who come to encounter God but not their fellow Christians. There is the 10 o'clock handclapping jamboree for parents and children where there is plenty of encounter with one another, but not much reverence and awe. At 6.30 in the evening it is the turn for youth culture. It is also the case that some congregations are situated in areas, such as housing estates, which are predominantly monocultural.

On the other hand we have seen (pages 41–43) that the overcoming of barriers and the mixing of people from all backgrounds is an integral part of the gospel message. A church cannot otherwise be a sign and foretaste of the kingdom. The most extreme form of homogeneity was demonstrated in South Africa in those denominations which had separate white and black congregations. The balance between being homogeneous and multicultural is paralleled by the need to be both 'local' and 'catholic' or universal; a congregation needs to become identified with its local culture while at the same time being open to an interchange of insights and ideas from the wider church. One line of answer is to recognise the need for homogenous approaches in evangelism, but to ensure that nurture and discipleship groups for those who profess faith are multi-cultural. Another approach is to allow 'cells' which are mono-cultural, but to ensure that 'congregations' and 'celebrations' are multi-cultural.

## Structures shaped by mission strategy

Too often strategy is shaped by structures rather than the other way round. The former Anglican bishop of São Paulo, the Rt Rev Sumio Takatsu, once used the analogy of the towel used to wipe the disciples' feet in the Upper Room (Jn 13). As a towel shapes itself to the foot, so structures and programmes must be shaped to the mission needs of the local context and culture. We have seen in this chapter how the people of God need to reject a 'compound mentality' and to be prepared not only to gather for worship, fellowship and teaching but also to be dispersed into the society. The church's structures must be shaped in such a way as to support individual members in their specific work and witness and to enable cells of Christians to engage with each local community. Only in this way will sympathy and solidarity be possible.

In the next chapter we look at the particular theological and practical issues raised as we relate to members of other faith communities.

Material for discussion and action on issues arising from this chapter will be found on page 189.

## Notes

1. Howard Snyder, *The Problem of Wineskins* (IVP: Illinois, 1976), especially Chapter 4.
2. For example the Universities and Colleges Christian Fellowship.

3. John Finney, *Finding Faith Today* (Bible Society: Swindon, 1992)

4. Jack Burton, *The Gap* (SPCK: London, 1991), p 28.

5. *The Church for Others* (WCC: Geneva, 1968), p 83.

6. *Ibid*, p 29.

7. Quoted in Thomas H McAlpine, *By Word, Work and Wonder: Cases in Holistic Mission* (MARC Publications: Monrovia, California, 1995), p 94.

8. Margaret Hebblethwaite, *Basic is Beautiful* (Fount: London, 1993), p 28.

9. *Ibid*.

10. *Ibid*, p 34.

11. *Ibid*, p 35.

12. John Reader, *Local Theology* (SPCK: London, 1994), pp 6–7.

13. An example illustrated in McAlpine, *op cit*, p 97.

14. See, for example, the guidebook by Ralph Neighbour, *Where Do We Go From Here?* (Touch Publications: Houston, Texas, 1990).

# CHAPTER EIGHT

# CHURCH, MOSQUE AND TEMPLE

*Good News for All Faiths?*

The skylines in many British cities have seen dramatic changes. Back-to-back terraced housing gave way to high rise blocks of flats and then as the problems of high-rise living were recognised many blocks were demolished for lower-level housing. Meanwhile, church towers and spires were joined by the domes and pinnacles of mosques and Hindu temples, signalling the fact that Britain is now a multi-faith society. The Victorians experienced other religions at a safe distance in 'heathen lands afar', through the eyes of missionaries and colonial soldiers and administrators. Now Muslims, Hindus, Sikhs and others live in the next town, the next street or next door. They bring a new spiritual dimension to a nation where many have become detached from their religious roots.

The 1950s, 60s and 70s saw migrants from the West Indies, Africa and Asia recruited to provide labour for hospitals, factories and transport. Many who came were Muslims, Hindus, Buddhists or Sikhs, but some came from a Christian background. It is important however to distinguish between colour, race, nationality and religion. Many 'blacks' are British by birth, while the majority of migrants today are 'white'. People visiting from door to door in London can encounter black Asian Christians, white Anglo-Saxon Buddhists and Muslims, and black British Christians.

Awareness of other faiths has increased through travel, television and the press, though portrayal has sometimes been distorted. The word 'Muslim', for example, is nearly always linked in parts of the press with the word 'fundamentalist'. The impression given is that all Muslims are militant extremists.

Because 'other religions' are often in the news, it is seldom realised that they are a relatively small proportion of the British population – under 5%.

However the importance and influence of adherents of 'other faiths' is well out of proportion to their size. The presence of other faiths forces Christians to think through afresh their understanding of the basic doctrines of the nature of God, of the person of Jesus Christ and of the way of salvation.

Although this chapter comes last it is one of the most important and although the above illustrations are drawn from the British scene the principles which follow have general application.

In any religion there is often a significant difference between the official teaching of that faith and what its followers actually believe. In befriending and entering discussion with followers of other faiths it is important to recognise that beliefs and opinions will differ considerably. This is so within the Christian churches as well, and even more so among those who call themselves Christians without attending church.

It is also important to recognise that we may have false assumptions as to what others believe. A minister was visiting a hospital ward and came across a Muslim leader who had been admitted with a broken pelvis. He asked the minister to pray for him. The minister hesitated and explained that his prayer would be in the name of Jesus. 'I know, I know. Jesus raised the dead. What is a broken pelvis to him?' The minister assumed that the Muslim was on the verge of becoming a Christian but the Qur'an teaches that Jesus as a prophet can bring healing, without being divine. Only sensitive and careful listening and dialogue will bring a clear understanding of others' beliefs.

The relativism and pluralism spawned by the Enlightenment

and described in Chapter 6 has already raised the question as to whether Christianity can be the only way. The presence of other faith communities has increased the doubts. It is easy to dismiss other faiths when they are far from our shores; it is less easy when we encounter a warmth, friendship, spirituality and dedication among Muslims and Hindus in our streets which contradict the caricatures we possess.

The launch of the Decade of Evangelism in 1991 was therefore a crisis point. Were the churches going to evangelise Muslims and Jews, for example? Some church leaders emphasised that their priority was to lapsed Christians and to those who have no faith, but not primarily or not at all to those of other faiths. Others argued that the good news was for all.

In recent years Christians who have engaged in the debate over the status of other faiths have been described as being in one of three categories:

the Pluralist
the Exclusivist
the Inclusivist

These categories have also been described as labelling other religions as 'right', 'wrong' and 'half-right'![1] As we shall see, each category includes a spectrum of opinion and the boundaries between them are more than a little blurred. Many interfaith activists are unhappy with them. It will therefore be helpful to introduce four sub-categories – extreme and moderate exclusivism, and moderate and broad inclusivism. The overlap between the different categories is set out in diagram form on page 168. Space does not permit more than an outline sketch of each position, but fuller expositions can be found elsewhere.[2]

*The pluralist position*

An old and popular illustration of the pluralist position is that the different religions are equivalent to a number of paths up a mountain. Each religion is a valid path to ultimate truth; the starting points, however, depend on factors of culture, history and geography and are therefore different. As with any analogy, this illustration has its defects; one is that a person can only travel up one mountain path at a time, whereas it is possible to be committed to more than one religion. Perhaps a better analogy is that of a shopping mall which has Indian, Chinese, French and Italian restaurants. There will be factors of birth, background, culture and taste that affect our choice of restaurant, but in theory any will serve the purpose of providing the calories the body needs, and there is no reason why a person should not transfer from one to another.

The mountain path analogy has been popular in the West because it suited the culture of secularisation which is tolerant of anything except intolerance. We can hold any view so long as we do not hold it too intensely. It also addresses the problem that our place of birth and upbringing undoubtedly affects which faith we profess. We are more likely to be at least a nominal Christian if we are brought up in the West, and more likely to be a Hindu if we are brought up in parts of India. In defining pluralism, Alan Race has described each response to God's revealing and redeeming activity in history as 'partial, incomplete, unique', representing different 'culturally focused perceptions of the one ultimate divine reality'.[3]

A leading exponent of the pluralist position is Professor John Hick who has spoken of the need for a 'Copernican' revolution. Scientists no longer believe that the earth is the centre of the universe, and by analogy Christians should no longer believe that their faith is at the centre. Rather it is one of the faiths orbiting round 'ultimate reality'. Pluralists speak of moving from a Christo-centric world to a 'Theocentric', or God-centred one, though many now speak of 'ultimate reality' rather than 'God' in order to include those forms of Buddhism which are effectively 'non-theistic'.

Many but not all pluralists argue that in terms of the truth all religions are on a similar level. Sometimes the term 'a wider ecumenism' is used – we should now include all faiths and not just all Christian denominations as part of our fellowship of faith.[4]

Pluralism is the position most difficult to square with New Testament teaching, though many pluralists would argue that such a statement is unfair in that the Bible shows no knowledge of Hinduism, Buddhism or Chinese religion, and the New Testament was written before Islam or Sikhism emerged. It is therefore argued that it is not always possible to apply biblical teaching directly to contemporary faiths. Even modern Judaism is not the faith of the first-century.

Critics of those pluralists who speak of an 'ultimate reality' claim that it is difficult to envisage such a vague entity becoming an attractive alternative to the historical Jesus of Nazareth or to the gods of other faiths.

## The exclusivist position

The exclusivist stands at the opposite end of the spectrum to the pluralist. This position argues from the New Testament that salvation can only be found in Jesus Christ. Emphasis is laid on Christ's words 'I am the way and the truth and the life. No one comes to the Father except through me' (Jn 14:6), and on Peter's words 'Salvation is found in no one else, for there is no other name under heaven given to men by which we must be saved' (Acts 4:12). Jesus Christ is unique as the Son of God who died and rose again to bring us salvation; this salvation is a free gift from God to those who repent and believe in him.

This *excludes*, therefore, all other faiths as vehicles of salvation.

The *extreme exclusivist* will argue that there is no truth to be found in other religions and that they are demonic in origin. Evangelism towards those of other faiths is therefore a matter of proclamation rather than dialogue. We have little or nothing to learn from them and our task is to expose error and to proclaim the truth as it is in Christ. For the extreme exclusivist, the only people who can receive salvation are those who overtly and consciously commit themselves to Jesus Christ in repentance and faith. All others are condemned.

## Moderate exclusivism

Many in the exclusivist category would, however, want to take a more moderate position. They draw attention to the historical doctrine known as 'general revelation'. This doctrine teaches that the Spirit of Christ is active in the world at large, revealing truth and inspiring goodness. The Apostle Paul argued in his letter to the Romans (eg Rom 1:18–20 and 2:12–16) that the nature of God and his moral standards are revealed to all. Indeed no one would ever come to faith if the Spirit were not active outside the church in bringing conviction of human sin and divine goodness (Jn 16:8–11). Therefore other faiths cannot be wholly wrong and of the devil. The moderate exclusivist will welcome, for example, the Muslim's dedication, the Sikh reverence for life and the Jewish emphasis on worship in the home.

However some exclusivists claim that truth or goodness is to be found in individual members of other faith communities rather than in the religious system to which they adhere. That distinction is a difficult one to press. The Spirit of Christ is active not only in individuals, but also in belief systems and structures.

Moderate exclusivists will also acknowledge that while conscious faith in Christ is normally a condition of receiving salvation there are exceptions. One category of exception found in the New Testament is that of Abraham and other Old Testament believers. The argument in Chapter 4 of Romans is that Abraham was justified and received salvation in Christ, but without a conscious knowledge of him. A moderate exclusivist is prepared to extend this exception to some members of other faiths who have never heard the good news of Jesus Christ, and have therefore never rejected him. This extension raises a number of further questions. What if some who have rejected

Christ have in fact rejected a false or distorted 'Christ' – the Christ of the Crusades, for example?

A moderate exclusivist may be prepared to conceive that a Muslim, for example, could receive salvation without a conscious knowledge of Christ. But this salvation is nevertheless 'in Christ', on the basis of his death and resurrection. It is available through repentance and faith, where the Muslim casts himself on the mercy of God. It cannot be on the basis of personal goodness or religious observance or on the grounds of the religion being followed.[5] The basis, in other words, is the one on which the publican was accepted, but the Pharisee rejected. Indeed that parable is a reminder that all religion, including Judaism and Christianity, can be a barrier to salvation if it is misused.

It is difficult to be dogmatic here as it is speculation which goes beyond the New Testament. In practical terms the biblical balance would seem to be to seek to bring the good news of Jesus Christ to all so that all have the opportunity of a conscious acceptance of him, while recognising that God alone can know the state of each human heart.

The case of Abraham is a reminder of the danger of lumping all 'other faiths' together. Whatever is felt about other faiths as a whole, Judaism is clearly in a special category. There are also some things which can be said about the three great monotheistic religions – Christianity, Judaism and Islam – which cannot be said about the others.

*The inclusivist position*

The midway position between pluralism and exclusivism is that of the inclusivist, who will argue that there is truth and goodness to be found in other faiths and this fact must be attributed to the Christ who is active in them. 'All truth is God's truth and Christ must therefore *include* all that is true in other faiths'.[6]

In some senses and to some degree the Spirit of God is present in each individual and in each religion, though ultimate truth has been finally and supremely revealed in Jesus Christ. A favourite inclusivist text is John 1:9 where it is said of Jesus Christ, the Logos or Word, 'The true light that gives light to every man was coming into the world.'

The papal document *Redemptoris Missio* speaks of 'everything that has been brought about in human beings by the Spirit who blows where he wills. Through dialogue the church seeks to uncover the "seeds of the Word", a "ray of that truth which enlightens all men"; these are found in individuals and in the religious traditions of mankind.'[7]

The three main positions, pluralism, exclusivism and inclusivism, are three spectrums within which a range of viewpoints can be found. Furthermore there is overlap between the spectrums, for example between moderate exclusivists and moderate inclusivists.

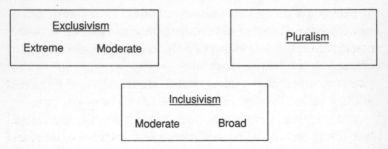

*Figure 17*

Although the exclusivist has been described as someone who holds that salvation is in Christ alone, this is a position which is also held by most inclusivists. The question is whether salvation is reserved for those who make an overt and conscious commitment to Jesus Christ.

Much of what has been said so far under inclusivism would be acceptable to moderate exclusivists. The differences at this point are more those of emphasis and practical application and less of principle and theory. In practice, the moderate inclusivist will be more positive about the teachings of other faiths, whereas the moderate exclusivist will give greater emphasis to their shortcomings and will regard the category of those who receive salvation in Christ without explicit faith in him as a narrow and exceptional one.

Some have defined their position as being in the overlap between exclusivism and inclusivism. Among those who have declared themselves to be in this overlap are Dr Chris Wright, principal of the evangelical All Nations Christian College.[8] The authors of the report 'Towards a Theology of Inter-faith dialogue'[9] describe themselves as being of the inclusivist position with an exclusivist loyalty to Jesus Christ. This view is open to a spectrum of interpretation, but at least underlines the difficulties of these categories.

## Is there salvation in other faiths?

The moderate exclusivist will argue that it is possible for those of other faiths to receive revelation, but not salvation within other faiths;[10] the definition of salvation implied is that described on pages 83–84. But some inclusivists speak in terms of other faiths being vehicles of salvation: salvation is always to be found in Christ, but not solely in the church or in Christianity.

The Church of England's Doctrine Commission has argued that 'God can and does work in people of other religions, and indeed within other religions . . . people are enabled to live better lives through loyally following other faiths, and this must mean that God is at work in these faiths, even if it cannot determine the question whether these faiths have value for ultimate salvation or not.'[11] The Anglican Bishops at the 1988 Lambeth Conference argued, 'People sometimes fear that to affirm the presence of any encounter with God outside of Christianity is to imply that any truth to be found there may, in its own right, be "saving truth". We wish to affirm that the only "truth" which has saving power is *God*.'[12]

Some are happy to speak of God as engaged in 'saving work'

in and through other faiths, but would be hesitant to say that those faiths are vehicles of salvation.

Many inclusivists speak in terms of Christ fulfilling some of the hopes and aspirations not only of Judaism, but of other faiths as well. Bishop Michael Nazir-Ali has argued that 'each group which has a language, a culture and a religious tradition has a salvation history,' and that just as Christ was the fulfilment of the salvation history of Judaism so there is a sense in which he can be a fulfilment of the salvation history of other faiths.[13] But Bishop Michael is careful to say that 'what constitutes a salvation history can . . . only be determined when there is a normative Salvation History'.[14]

Further along the inclusivist spectrum and in the sub-category of *broad inclusivism* comes the Roman Catholic theologian Karl Rahner. He became famous for his use of the phrase 'anonymous Christians' to describe those who had found truth and salvation in Christ, but did not know or acknowledge him. A Hindu, for example, could be saved by Christ, but through the sacraments of Hinduism. It sometimes appears that those who refer to Christ in this way are speaking of a cosmic, a-historical Christ who has little connection with the historical Jesus. The Logos or Word of John Chapter 1 has sometimes been described as the *Logos Spermatikos* the 'scattered or seminal word'. We can say that the eternal Logos or Word of God, Christ in his divine nature, is active in ways that go beyond the life and ministry of the historical Jesus and that the historical Jesus does not exhaust the truth of God. The Logos or Word of God has been active prior to the Incarnation from eternity. But the Incarnation permanently brought together the two natures of Christ – human and divine. It is not possible to conceive of new truth being revealed in other religions which is inconsistent with what we know of the historical Jesus. To put it another way, the historical Jesus revealed in the Scriptures must be normative, the Logos cannot be revealed in other religions in ways which are contrary to the revelation in Jesus of Nazareth.

Today it is more common to attribute the presence of goodness and truth in other faiths and in the world at large to the work of the Holy Spirit – though again the doctrine of the Trinity means that we think in terms of the Spirit *of Christ* and therefore cannot conceive of 'truths' being discovered in other faiths which are inconsistent with the truth revealed through the historical Jesus. The Holy Spirit is the Spirit of Jesus Christ and he has the task of glorifying him. 'The touchstone of the quality of the Spirit's activity in the life of any person, whether Christian or not, is the evidence of a Christ-like spirit.'[15]

## The three categories summarised

The three categories of pluralism, exclusivism and inclusivism can be summarised as follows:

Pluralism – salvation through all faiths.
Extreme exclusivism – salvation through overt faith in Jesus Christ.
Moderate exclusivism – salvation in Jesus Christ and normally through overt faith.
Moderate inclusivism – salvation in Jesus Christ.
Broad inclusivism – salvation in the cosmic Christ within other faiths.

The tension for the moderate positions is to safeguard both the uniqueness and the universality of Christ. I would be happy to describe myself as a moderate exclusivist, in terms of the definitions above, but I have sympathy with those who take a moderate inclusivist position. Bishop Lesslie Newbigin illustrates the complexities of definition by declaring his position as 'exclusivist in the sense that it affirms the unique truth of the revelation of Jesus Christ, but it is not exclusivist in the sense of denying the possibility of the salvation of the non-Christian. It is inclusivist in the sense that it refuses to limit the saving grace of God to the members of the Christian church, but it rejects the inclusivism which regards the non-Christian religions as vehicles of salvation. It is pluralist in the sense of acknowledging the gracious work of God in the lives of all human beings, but it rejects a pluralism which denies the uniqueness and decisiveness of what God has done in Jesus Christ.'[16]

Another way of defining the differences is to distinguish four approaches to evangelism:

**Evangelism as inappropriate** for members of other faiths. For the pluralist all religions are valid and it is therefore inappropriate to invite those of other faiths to consider the possibility of becoming Christians.

**Evangelism as necessarily destructive** of other faiths. The extreme exclusivist viewpoint.

**Evangelism as largely constructive**, building on the beliefs of other faiths. The broad inclusivist view.

**Evangelism as both challenging and constructive**, the approach of the moderate exclusivist and the moderate inclusivist.

## What can we learn from the Old Testament?

A number of Bible references have already been examined, but there are one or two others that need to be addressed at this point.

There are many examples in the Old Testament where God works in the lives of those who do not belong to his people. Naaman is cleansed of leprosy and is allowed to continue to accompany his master to the temple of Rimmon (2 Kings 5:1–19). In the book of Jonah the sailors seem to have a deeper spirituality than the prophet himself (Jon 1). Cyrus, king of Babylon, is described as God's servant (Is 44:28–45:7). The prophet Malachi describes God as being willing to accept worship from the people of every nation (Mal 1:11) 'In every place incense is offered to my name and a pure offering.'[17]

It is clear from these examples that awareness and experience of God was not limited to his people. In at least two cases God speaks to his people through 'outsiders'. Melchizedek is paid tithes by Abraham and is seen as a type of the Messiah (Gen 14:18–20 and Heb 5:6). Balaam receives messages from God (Num 22–24) to pass on to the people of Israel.

## The New Testament

There are many examples in the New Testament of God's activity among those who were not members of his people. When Paul arrives in Athens he looks beyond the 'tourist attractions' and is distressed at the fact that the city is full of idols (Acts 17:16). After preaching Christ in the synagogue and in the market place, he is summoned to the city council, the Areopagus, to give an account of his teaching. He begins by referring to an altar he had noticed with the inscription 'to an unknown god'. While he corrects the errors of the Athenians' beliefs and worship, he positively declares, 'What you worship as something unknown I am going to proclaim to you' (Acts 17:23). As far as he can he builds on the beliefs they had, and it could be argued that he presents Christ as the fulfilment of their hopes and aspirations.

An equally interesting passage is Acts 10 where a Roman centurion, Cornelius, is told by an angel that his prayers have been heard by God. The comment by the Apostle Peter is that God 'accepts men from every nation who fear him and do what is right' (Acts 10:35). In what sense, however, are people like Cornelius 'acceptable' to God? This may well fall short of full 'salvation' and it is important to note that Peter goes on to share with Cornelius and his friends 'the good news of peace through Jesus Christ'. Furthermore Cornelius is probably a 'godfearer' – an enquirer on the edges of Judaism wanting to explore faith, rather than a follower of another religion. However the main reason why Luke includes this story is probably not so much to describe the conversion of Cornelius, as the 'conversion' of

Peter to a recognition that the gospel is for all. This passage would support a moderate exclusivism or inclusivism, but not pluralism or an extreme exclusivism that denied all knowledge of God outside the people of God.

It is important to note here two significant events from the ministry of Jesus. The parable of the Good Samaritan deliberately highlights the goodness demonstrated in the adherent of 'another faith': the good man is the one furthest from orthodox faith. The encounter with the Samaritan woman can be read as seeking to break down some of the barriers between those of different faiths and as a concern to transcend religious differences (Jn 4:19–24). All religion must be judged by whether the worshippers worship God in spirit and truth.

*Faiths in contact*

Individuals and congregations who begin from a conservative or exclusivist position often find that their attitudes are softened or modified as a result of actual contact with Muslims, Hindus or others. One inner-city church majored on traditional direct evangelism, but began to develop an openness to other religious views and to the social needs of people in the area as friendships were developed.

Social contact can lead on to discussion about faith. Sometimes opportunities for such discussions arise through 'mixed marriages'. An English Christian woman married a Shi'ite Muslim man in Iran and visited an Islamic scholar to get advice over cultural scruples involved in entertaining friends. The conversation moved onto matters of faith and at the end the scholar said, 'The great difference between you and me is that when you have prayed to God, you can acknowledge that you have experienced God personally, whereas my faith teaches me that this is impossible.' It should be noted in passing that this would not be true of all branches of Islam.

In approaches to other faiths it is important to compare 'best' with 'best', not to compare the ideals of Christianity with the worst practices of another faith.

## Language

Particular issues arise when the gospel is brought to a country or people group for the first time. It needs translating into the ideas and language of the area. The missionary has to find words that will express 'God', Spirit' and 'faith'. Whether he or she will coin new words or use words already available from another faith will depend on the context.

Arabic-speaking Christians in Muslim areas use the word *Allah* to describe the Christian God. The decision has to be made whether adherents of other faiths are worshipping a false god, or whether they are seeking to worship the true God, but with an erroneous or limited understanding of his true nature and character. Clearly the latter is the case with Judaism and many would say the same about Islam. The Rev Graham Kings has argued that the 'High God' of some African traditional religions can be seen in this way.[18] Contrary to earlier belief, several modern anthropologists have demonstrated that early tribal beliefs have normally centred on one god and that polytheism is a later development.

## Dialogue

The approach frequently recommended in contacting those of other faiths is that of dialogue. It is a word, as will be demonstrated below, with a range of meanings, but it normally implies a concern to listen, to understand and to receive as well as to give. Christian pluralists, and some inclusivists, will approach dialogue with a Hindu, for example, in a completely open-ended way. The end result can never be foreseen and the Christian may become a Hindu or the Hindu a Christian. By contrast the extreme exclusivist will see dialogue purely as a tool for evangelism; he tries to listen and understand, not with the expectation of discovering new truth, but simply in order to find what will be the most effective language and approach for presenting the Christian gospel. Dialogue in this sense is a tool of persuasion. In between comes the inclusivist, and some exclusivists, who do not enter dialogue with the expectation of wavering from their basic commitment to Christ but are open to the possibility of deepening and extending their understanding, not only of the other faith but also of truths common to both faiths that they have not fully appreciated before, and to understand more fully their own faith. Bishop Tom Butler and his wife Barbara have said that, 'This encounter with those of other faiths can be a 'mirror' which teaches us more about our own spiritual journey by illuminating and deepening our approach to God through Jesus Christ in the power of the Holy Spirit.'[19]

There are a large number of insights we can learn from other faiths. As long ago as 1928 the International Missionary Conference held in Jerusalem spoke positively about 'that sense of the Majesty of God and the consequent reverence in worship, which are conspicuous in Islam' and 'the deep sympathy for the world's sorrow . . . which are at the heart of Buddhism.'[20]

David Bosch argued that true dialogue presupposes commitment, otherwise it is superfluous. 'An "unprejudiced" approach is not merely impossible but would actually subvert dialogue.' On the other hand 'we go expecting to meet the God who has preceded us and has been preparing people within the context of their culture and convictions'. We do not have the Holy Spirit 'in our pocket' – 'he accompanies us and also comes toward us.'[21] Dr Christopher Lamb has described the ideal as 'a committed mind, but not a closed mind'.[22]

The World Council of Churches, meeting at Uppsala in 1968, argued that 'a Christian's dialogue with another implies neither a denial of the uniqueness of Christ, nor any loss of his own commitment to Christ, but rather that a genuinely Christian approach to others must be human, personal, relevant and humble.'[23]

Although the word 'proclamation' is the one most often associated with evangelism the Apostle Paul uses the approaches of discussion, debate and dialogue a remarkable number of times. Examples can be found at Thessalonica (Acts 17:2) as well as at Athens (Acts 17:17), and Corinth (Acts 18:4). The NIV normally translates *dialegomai* as 'reasoning' – no doubt there were times when discussion turned into argument, but this may not have been Paul's fault if this was so! Paul's approach to dialogue was clearly not a pluralist one, but may have been on the boundaries of exclusivism and inclusivism.

One of the many lessons that can be learnt from our contact with those of other faiths is the importance of listening and discovery through dialogue – an approach that is important in evangelism among those who are secularists or humanists as well. John Stott has commended dialogue in these words: 'It is once more the challenge of the Incarnation, to renounce evangelism by inflexible slogans, and instead to involve ourselves sensitively in the real dilemmas of men . . . Dialogue is a token of genuine Christian love, because it indicates our steadfast resolve to rid our minds of the prejudices and caricatures which we may entertain about other people; to struggle to listen through their ears and look through their eyes so as to grasp what prevents them from hearing the gospel and seeing Christ; to sympathise with them in all their doubts, fears and "hang-ups".'[24]

The beautiful Easter story of the walk to Emmaus (Lk 24:13–35) demonstrates a form of dialogue where Jesus comes alongside two disciples, asks what they are discussing, and draws out from them their hopes, fears and uncertainties. He then presents the prophecies of resurrection from the Old Testament Scriptures, but at the end of the journey waits for an invitation before entering their home and revealing himself. This sensitivity is the opposite of aggressive or manipulative evangelism.

Dialogue cannot be neutral, and it is not wrong to witness

attractively and persuasively provided the integrity of the other person is respected. There will be differences from individual to individual and from one faith community to another. Islam, for example, is a missionary faith but modern Judaism is not. In one inner-city area dialogue had to be developed slowly because some of the Muslim groups were actively campaigning for Islam and some Muslim children would call out to Christians 'We don't like your God!'

Because the Jewish community in Britain and in some other countries is declining in numbers and because of their history of persecution, climaxing in the Holocaust, there has to be special sensitivity in Christian-Jewish dialogue.

### 'The dialogue of life'

Very often bridges of friendship and trust have to be built before there can be sharing of faith. An important dimension to this is what has been described as 'the dialogue of life' where there is a sharing of everyday joys and struggles, with perhaps a developing partnership in tackling the needs of the local community. One inner-city church has had a large but crumbling building demolished and a new complex built that provides a medical clinic, an advice centre for housing and community needs, sheltered accommodation and other facilities for all races and faiths. This dialogue of life is important in its own right and not just as a prelude to the sharing of faith.

### Visions, dreams and healings

The emphasis on dialogue might give the false impression that most people come to faith in Christ as a result of intellectual discussion. There are many instances of Muslims and Hindus coming to such faith through a vision, a dream or an experience of healing. Jesus is described in the Qur'an as a prophet who heals, so an experience of healing, as we saw on page 162, does not necessarily imply faith in the Christian sense. But sometimes it does.

Three Muslims were baptised in a west London church because one of them had received a vision of Christ. A Hindu appealed to Jesus as one of the Avitars; he received a vision of Christ and later believed.

One Roman Catholic priest trained his laity to befriend their Hindu neighbours and to offer prayer for their needs. They would use Hindu terminology and pray in the name of Jesus. Many received answers to prayer and some came to faith in Christ.

## Continuity or discontinuity?

A number of important questions arise when a man or woman of another faith becomes a Christian. We have seen in Chapter 6 that we need to distinguish between the gospel and culture, but there are particular problems when culture and religion are interwoven, as so often is the case. Michele Guinness, a Christian author who comes from a Jewish background, realised the need to retain, for example, the family worship emphasis of her Jewish childhood.[25] There are a number of Christian synagogues of 'Messianic Jews' created to help those Jews who become Christians but do not want to give up their Jewish culture. Similarly Martin Robinson speaks of those in Islamic countries who have become Christian but have sought to retain Islamic culture.[26]

Should a Sikh convert put aside the symbols of the Sikh faith? Can he now attend Sikh wedding or funeral ceremonies for members of his own family? One such convert, now a Christian minister, believes that the God he worships in church is the same as the God worshipped by other members of his family in the Gurdwara. He still wears the Sikh steel bracelet. 'My Christian loyalty inspires my respect for my Sikh roots, rather than leading me to reject them.'[27]

One of the many joys for Christians in relating to people of other faiths is a deepening in their understanding not only of that other faith but also of their own faith. The principles of dialogue which develop are relevant to most evangelism contexts, whether nominal Christian, religious or secular.

## Common religion

Many of the theological and practical issues that arise in the relationship between Christianity and other faiths could apply to some extent in the relationship to 'common religion', to 'New Age', to new religious movements such as Scientology and even to secular humanism.

The description 'common religion' is often used of those who are not adherents of any major religion and yet have some faith in God and a sense of 'belonging' to the Christian church. Although only 14% of the adult population of Great Britain are church members, 34% of the population claim to believe in a personal God, and as many as 71% 'believe in God'. Fifty-four per cent define themselves as 'religious' and 57% 'need moments of prayer'.[28] In the United States, which has a much higher rate of church attendance, two-fifths say they experience God's presence on a daily basis and at the other end of the spectrum one-fifth say they have felt it once or twice in their lives.

Many in the West have a strong sense of identification with the Christian faith, but this sense of identification is not matched by participation in the life of the church. This is a phenomenon which occurs with most institutions today. There are those who identify with a particular football team without attending a match, and those who identify with a political party without going to any political meetings.

In the case of 'common religion' there will often be participation at moments of national or local crisis, such as the Hillsborough football disaster in Sheffield in 1989 when ninety-four Liverpool football supporters died, or at key moments in family and personal life such as birth, marriage and death. In the days that followed the Hillsborough disaster, one million people visited the Liverpool football pitch to pay their respects.

We are indebted to Bishop John Finney for his research on how people come to faith,[29] but his research sample is taken from those who are members of churches. It is even more important to research those who make similar faith journeys without joining a church.

The relationship of 'believing and belonging' is complex. The figures given above show that many who do not belong in a participatory sense to the church, nevertheless have significant beliefs. On the other hand the Finney research shows that those who make a public profession of faith have been influenced less by dialogue about Christian beliefs: rather they have been drawn in through friendship with individual church members and by joining a group which includes church members and which acts as a bridge into the church. In this sense belonging comes before believing. Yet traditionally the approach to baptism has been to require a profession of belief before the candidate is allowed to belong. There are of course specific theological issues with regard to baptism which it is not appropriate to develop here, but baptism is often the occasion when the range of attitudes to common religion held by church leaders come to the surface. This range of attitudes has parallels with the spectrums of inclusivism and exclusivism.

There is not space here to develop further the particular issues raised by 'New Age', new religious movements or by common religion. This has been done elsewhere.[30] There are, however, a number of theological issues which are similar to those arising in connection with other faiths. Some see the beliefs of common religion, of humanism and of other philosophies as core foundation materials on which we can build; others see them as rubble to be cleared away[31] before the building blocks of Christian faith can be erected.

As described on page 172 some see evangelism in this context as necessarily destructive, some see it as constructive and yet others as both challenging and constructive.

*The importance of other faiths*

This chapter has underlined the importance of befriending members of other faith communities, not only because we desire to develop understanding and harmony in society, but because we believe we have much to learn from and to share with each other. Such encounters also help Christians to understand their own faith more fully.

The principles of listening, understanding and dialogue are valid for all evangelism – with those of other faiths, with those who have no faith, and with those whose beliefs can be described as belonging to either 'common' or 'implicit' religion.

Material for discussion and action on issues arising from this chapter will be found on page 190.

**Notes**

1. John Saxbee, *Liberal Evangelism* (SPCK: London, 1994), p 79.
2. The following publications give fuller expositions and include booklists:
   *Towards a Theology of Inter-Faith Dialogue* (Church House Publishing: London, 1986).
   *The Mystery of Salvation*, a report by the Doctrine Commission of the General Synod of the Church of England (Church House Publishing: London, 1995), see especially Chapter 7.
3. Alan Race, *Christians and Religious Pluralism* (Orbis: 1982), p 78.
4. This is sometimes justified by the fact that ecumenism in its root-meaning refers to the whole inhabited earth.
5. This is the argument used by a former chairman of the General Synod House of Laity of the Church of England – Sir Norman Anderson – 'multitudes of Jews . . . in Old

Testament times, turned to God in repentance, brought the prescribed sacrifice, and threw themselves on his mercy. It was not that they *earned* that mercy by their repentance and obedience, or that an animal sacrifice could ever avail to atone for human sin. It was that their repentance and faith . . . opened the gate as it were to . . . grace, mercy and forgiveness which he always longed to extend to them, and which was to be made for ever available at the cross . . . May we not believe, then, that the same would be true of the follower of some other religion in whose heart the God of all mercy had been working by his Spirit . . . and who had been enabled . . . to throw himself on the mercy of God?'
J N D Anderson, *Christianity and Other Religions* (IVP: Leicester, 1970), pp 101–102, quoted by Chris Sugden, *Christ's Exclusive Claims and Inter-Faith Dialogue* (Grove Books: Bramcote, Notts, 1985), pp 13–14.

6. A phrase used by Dr Chris Wright in defining inclusivism: see Chris Wright, *What's Unique about Jesus?* (Monarch: Crowborough, 1990), p 40.

7. *Redemptoris Missio* (Catholic Truth Society: London, 1991), paragraph 56.

8. Wright, *op cit*, p 59. In order to understand Dr Wright's position it is important to note the definitions he uses of exclusivism and inclusivism.

9. *Towards a Theology for Inter-Faith Dialogue* 2nd edition (Church House Publishing: London, 1986), p 35.

10. For example Dr Chris Wright, *op cit*, p 42.

11. *The Mystery of Salvation*, *op cit*, p 181.

12. *The Truth shall make you Free*, the Report of the 1988 Lambeth Conference (Church House Publishing: London, 1988), p 95.

13. *Frontiers in Muslim-Christian Encounter* (Regnum: Oxford, 1987), p 20.

14. *Towards a Theology for Inter-Faith Dialogue*, *op cit*, p 47.

15. *We believe in the Holy Spirit*, a report of the Doctrine

Commission of the Church of England (Church House Publishing: London, 1991), p 12.

16. Lesslie Newbigin, *The Gospel in a Pluralist Society* (SPCK: London, 1989), p 182, quoted in *Multi-Faith Worship?* (CHP: London, 1992), p 17.

17. Revised Standard Version. The future tense used in the NIV is less likely, though if accurate would substantiate the exclusivist argument that this verse refers to the end time.

18. Graham Kings, *Facing Mount Kenya: Reflections on the Bible and African Traditional Religion*. An article in *Anvil* magazine Vol 4, No 2, 1987, Cambridge, p 127.

19. Barbara and Tom Butler, *Just Mission* (Mowbray: London, 1993), p 9.

20. David Bosch, *Transforming Mission* (Orbis: New York, 1991), p 480.

21. *Ibid*, p 484.

22. From an article in *Ambassador*, the journal of the Church of England Board of Mission (Summer 1995)

23. *World Council of Churches Uppsala Report II*, (WCC: Geneva), paragraph 6.

24. J R W S Stott, *Christian Mission in the Modern World* (Falcon: London, 1975), p 81.

25. For example, Michele Guinness, *Child of the Covenant* (Hodder: London, 1985).

26. Martin Robinson, *The Faith of the Unbeliever* (Monarch: Crowborough, 1994), p 156.

27. *Good News in Our Times* (Church House Publishing: London, 1991), p 69.

28. 1990 figures published in Grace Davie's, *Religion in Britain since 1945* (Blackwell: Oxford, 1994), p 78.

29. John Finney, *Finding Faith Today* (Bible Society: Swindon, 1992).

30. In particular, Davie, *op cit*, and Robinson, *op cit*.

31. An illustration used in Saxbee, *op cit*, p 110.

# EPILOGUE

On the evening of that first day of the week, when the disciples were together, with the doors locked for fear of the Jews, Jesus came and stood among them and said 'Peace be with you!' After he said this he showed them his hands and his side . . . Again Jesus said, 'Peace be with you! As the Father has sent me, I am sending you.' And with that he breathed on them and said, 'Receive the Holy Spirit. If you forgive anyone his sins they are forgiven; if you do not forgive them, they are not forgiven.' (Jn 20:19–23).

This Easter story neatly summarises our call to evangelise. Those who are disciples of Christ are called to continue Christ's mission – he provides the model, the motivation and the power to share good news.

The 'sending' is a continuous activity – in fact we join with him in his continuing mission to the world. He offers us his Spirit to fill us with his compassion, sensitivity and endurance. We are called to listen as well as speak, to engage in an 'Emmaus' style of evangelism (page 177).

The word 'peace' must have been more than a formal word of greeting – it was an offer of reconciliation to the group which had denied and deserted him in his greatest hour of need, a reminder to us that none of us is worthy to take on his work, and need the mercy, grace and peace that he offers. Ultimately peace or 'shalom' represents the vision of a new creation where men, women and the environment are transformed into what God has intended them to be (pages 44–46).

But before he gives the disciples his commission he shows them the scars in his hands and side. This was firstly to help them recognise who he was. But it must also have been designed both to emphasise the ground of their forgiveness and to demonstrate the costly style of mission to which we are called – one of identifying with a suffering world.

James Shillito was the poet of the battlefields of the First World War and wrote a poem under the title *Jesus of the Scars*. The last verse says:

> The other gods were strong; but thou wast weak;
> They rode, but thou didst stumble to a throne;
> But to our wounds only God's wounds can speak,
> And not a god has wounds, but thou alone.[1]

We must be careful not to attribute impotence to God, but nor must we portray a God who is immune from suffering. He was ready to give up his security and protection to make himself vulnerable.

'To be in the places where people hurt most is the only place to be.'[2]

**Notes**

1. Quoted by Tom Smail, *Windows on the Cross* (Darton, Longman and Todd: London, 1995), p 66.
2. Words of a mother of a child at Dunblane Primary School, March 1996 – see Introduction.

# ISSUES FOR DISCUSSION
# AND ACTION

The following issues are listed under chapter headings, but are interconnected and therefore transferable.

## Introduction

1. Invite members of a group to list a number of definitions of evangelism. Write them up on a flip-chart or overhead projector. Discuss the advantages and limitations of each.
2. Does it really matter how we define evangelism?
3. In what ways have we failed to get involved in others' suffering? Is there any way in which our attitude has been like that of the American missionary?

## Chapter One: What Hope for Planet Earth?

1. Which of the potential catastrophes facing planet earth are most likely to happen?
2. Are there practical steps we can take to alert people of the dangers?
3. What changes to our lifestyle are needed?
4. The chapter lists six specific trends and counter-trends (pages 29–36) What examples of these trends can you find in your own experience and locality?

5. What effect should these trends have on our style and methods of evangelism?

## Chapter Two: Good News for a New Millennium

1. Which of the 'good news words' listed in this chapter are most relevant to the people and situations that you know? Are there others you could add?
2. Are there divisions or differences in your church or community where reconciliation is needed? How can it be brought about?
3. How can the right balance of unity and diversity be achieved within your church and community?

## Chapter Three: Pie in the Sky?

1. What social needs are there in your community? You may like to set up a group to identify members of your congregation who have contacts with local industry, shops, schools, hospitals, government and local authority offices etc and discuss needs with them.
2. Are there social need programmes that your church is (or should be) involved in? What about other churches in the area? Are there some projects which could be undertaken jointly?
3. How can such programmes be related to evangelism?
4. Investigate the courses and materials your church uses for evangelism and Christian nurture. How far do they have an adequate social dimension?
5. How far do these materials and the evangelistic talks and sermons that we usually hear challenge to costly discipleship as opposed to offering 'cheap grace'?

## Chapter Four: Healing, Suffering and Hope

1. Are there ways in which a healing ministry can be developed in your church? If you already have one, are there ways in which it can be developed further?

2. How far do our church programmes, including its healing ministry, help us to look outward rather than inward?

3. How far, in the experience of the group, has suffering been a bridge to evangelism rather than a barrier?

*Chapter Five: The Lord is my Shop Steward*

1. Ask each member of the group to write in their own words a brief explanation of the gospel. Discuss in pairs how far the language used would be intelligible to those outside the church and what words and phrases could be used to make the explanation clearer.

2. The chapter gives a number of emphases needed for a 'post-modern' style of evangelism (pages 117–121). How far does the group agree with them? Are there any that should be added?

3. Discuss how these approaches can be used in practice, especially the emphases on affirmation, dialogue, process and experience.

*Chapter Six: God's Pilot Project*

1. Visit a church of a different tradition. Note the difficulties and adjustments you face and whether you are made to feel welcome and accepted. Now go back to your own church and try to see the service through the eyes of a visitor (better still, bring one with you!) What changes need to be made to make the worship more intelligible?

2. Discuss how far your welcome strategy is adequate; does it go beyond the initial welcome?

3. Imagine your congregation is lifted up and re-planted in a rural part of Africa which is French speaking. What changes will be needed to your worship and programme?

*Chapter Seven: Body Shapes*

1. Are there parts of your local area where there is little contact with the church? It would be helpful to plot members' homes

on a map and also to undertake an 'audit' to show the age and social profile of both the congregation and also of the area to see which groups are missing.[1]
2. What bridges into the community are already in place and how effective are they? What new ones could be built? Would a church plant be helpful?
3. Look at the data produced in answer to question 1 under Chapter 3. Add to this the involvement of church members outside your area. How can church members be better equipped and supported in relating their faith to work, leisure pursuits and community affairs? Would a work or community related cell be helpful?

*Chapter Eight: Church, Mosque and Temple*

1. Seek to discover what other faith communities, if any, there are in your area.
2. Undertake a survey to find out what people in your area believe.
3. Explore ways of building bridges for friendship and eventually dialogue.

## Notes

1. Material can be found in John Finney's, *The Well Church* (CPAS: Leamington Spa, 1991)